THE *Networking* REVOLUTION

Five Ways Women Are Changing Their Lives Through Home Business Ownership

Jessica Higdon & April O'Leary

Download Your
FREE COPY of
The Home Business Matrix at
TheNetworkingRevolution.com

The Networking Revolution

Five Ways Women Are Changing Their Lives Through Home Business Ownership
©2015 Jessica Higdon and April O'Leary

Print ISBN: 978-1-937660-87-1
eBook ISBN: 978-1-937660-88-8

Published by The Networking Revolution

For information on quantity discounts and bonus gifts please visit:
TheNetworkingRevolution.com

Cover Design By: Christine E. Dupre
Interior Design By: Lisa Thomson
Back Cover Photography: Julie Renner Photography

Also by Jessica Higdon

Top Earner Recruting Secrets:
How to Recruit More Reps Into Your MLM

Also by April O'Leary

Ride the Wave:
Journey to Peaceful Living

Focus on You, Your Needs Matter Too:
6 Lessons to Help You Find Happiness
and Take Better Care of You

*To all of the women who have
changed their lives through
starting a home business.
This is for you!*

Acknowledgements

We would like to thank the following people for their efforts to support us as we worked together to complete this project. Whether that was through reading a rough draft copy, offering ideas for improvement, proofreading, editing, sharing a success story or most importantly believing in the vision to create a unified group of home business owners who support one another, we are so grateful. A success for one is a success for all.

For Careful Editing:
Marjorie Eichhorn
Emily Brown
Torrey Skloff

For Photography Set and Design:
Julie Renner Photography
Kristina Jay

For Skilled Book Design:
Christine Dupre
Hanne Moon
Lisa Thomson
Heritage Press Publications

For Critical Content Input:
Michael Clouse
Anthony McIntosh
James A. O'Leary

For Exceptional Admin and Marketing:
Kris Nicolas
Patricia Sweeney
Nick Haubner
Thomas Bouwman

For Generously Sharing Success Stories:
Rosalyn Powell
Tanya Aliza
Elexsis McCarthy
Lindsey Catarino
Cherie Rodriguez
Paulette Roy
Lora Ulrich
Lisa Wilber
Kelly Ellis-Neal
Danielle Russo-Slugh
Debbie Fox Sasek
Tracey Schwartz
Beth Leipold
Joy Vertz
Jessica Bowser Nelson

For Believing in Us:
Lisa Grossman
Eric and Marina Worre
All of Our Coaching Clients
Team Start Living
The Entire Top Earner Team –
love you guys

Jake and Nancy Kevorkian
Chris and Deloris Kent
Ian and Valerie Cordell
Lisa Sasevich
Maria Andros

And finally they would like to thank our families. Ray and Sabrina, Brandon and Ethan Higdon and Jim, Sadie, Molly and Amy O'Leary. This would not have been possible without you!

Table of Contents

Introduction April

Did you know someone starts a home-based business every ten seconds? It's true!

I'm April O'Leary, and I started my home-based life and business coaching practice in 2010. Back then I had no idea that most businesses take 3-5 years to become profitable and that 90% of businesses fail in the first five years. I don't say that to discourage you but rather to tell you there is an easier, more proven path you can travel to home business ownership. That is what this book will show you.

A little about me. I've been married since 2001 and I'm a mom of three girls ages 14, 12 and 8. I get up early to exercise on most days, am involved with the school's parent association and I work my business around my family's life. I have a B.A. in Elementary and Middle School Education and always thought I'd be a teacher. But life had other plans.

After being home with my kids for eight years and having weathered some personal challenges, which I share in my book Ride The Wave: Journey to Peaceful Living, I decided I wanted to help women live happier, healthier and wealthier lives. So I went back to school to get a life coaching certification and over the past five years I have had the privilege of coaching CEOs of companies, doctors, at-home moms and business owners between the ages of 24-75 to achieve the success they desire in their personal and professional lives.

Because I was building my business alone, I deliberately befriended other women business owners for support, went to conferences and took online courses so I could keep improving my skills. I learned how to develop websites, write and publish books, create my own online courses and I even put on two conferences for moms.

Then one afternoon while scrolling through the photos from the second *Happy Mom Conference* I noticed something. The vendors who filled the perimeter of the room were moms with direct sales businesses.

I saw a need that I could fill so I opened an online coaching group to provide weekly accountability specifically for women in direct sales called The Hive. Simultaneously I launched *Network Marketing TV* where I started interviewing top women leaders in the direct sales industry. It was then I realized we are right in the middle of a *Networking Revolution* and YOU can be a part of it!

This book showed up in your life for a reason. Inside you'll find a new and refreshing perspective on the Franchise-From-Home (FFH) industry, better known as Direct Selling or Network Marketing. We'll go through some of the myths that are perpetuated about network marketing that simply aren't true and we'll share, in solid numbers, both the Global and U.S. statistics.

You'll have the opportunity to see the five ways women are changing their lives through home-business ownership and you'll meet fourteen amazing women who have generously shared their success stories and are living lives they never dreamed possible. Special thanks to these women for their willingness to be included in this book!

Even if you have an existing business you can still incorporate the direct sales model into it as another revenue stream. I did and it's been a blessing for both my clients and me.

Take an hour to read this book cover to cover. Ask the person who gave it to you to share more about their business. Consider joining the thousands of women business owners who have said 'YES' to partnering with a company they love and are building a business from home in the nooks and crannies of their already busy lives.

Check out the resources section for more free offerings and business help.

My hope is that this book will become your go-to resource for supporting women business owners. Whether you choose to be a more conscious consumer or an intentional entrepreneur, there is something for you here.

I would love to help you build a business and life you love. I invite you to download the MP3 I created for you called *The Most Essential Ingredient to Home-Business Success* at apriloleary.com. You'll also receive the printable featured in Chapter 7 called "*Six Questions to Ask Yourself Every Week.*"

If you get value from this book, I encourage you to buy a few copies for friends and help spread the message. **It takes all of us working together to create a *Networking Revolution* in support of women entrepreneurs.** I'm all in. I hope you will be too!

Keep Buzzing,
April O'Leary
april@apriloleary.com

P.S. You are welcome to email me anytime. I would love to hear from you!

Introduction Jessica

From the time I was five years old I knew I wanted to be an entrepreneur. I just felt something in my bones and knew that I wasn't meant to work for someone else. Ever felt that way?

If you haven't, it's OK; this book is still for you. We will talk about where you fit in later on.

When I was 12, I started a business out of my middle school locker called "Locker Lockets." They were magnetic locker holders shaped like hearts that would hold little things you didn't want scattered all over your locker. I made them for $1.50 and sold them for $4. People loved them. I LOVED selling them. It was fun, fulfilling and quite profitable.

At 15 I toyed with the idea of starting my own jewelry business. My step-mom made amazing jewelry from beads, so I thought if she taught me how to do the same, I could sell them online! I always had new ideas to become independently wealthy, however somewhere along the way I lost the entrepreneurial spirit and thought I'd *get a job* like everyone else. I unconsciously began despising the salesperson and envied the entrepreneur because it was something I had always wanted to accomplish but hadn't done so.

Society played a huge role in my negativity. I always heard that sales people were "bad" or they were just trying to "take advantage" of you. So when a huge opportunity came along in the direct sales profession, I was totally closed to the idea. I immediately turned it down, like many people do, as if I knew everything there is to know about this particular industry. I thought I was happy where I was.

At the time I was broke and I was going to college full-time and working at a makeup counter part-time. I was also applying for every interview I could in my chosen field of marketing. After the tenth interview where someone was telling me I would start at a low pay, had "possible" room for growth and no benefits to start, I began to see that my options weren't as great as I thought.

Then I met someone who changed my life forever. He took me under his wing and showed me how amazing the network marketing profession could truly be. I decided to give this "*direct sales*" thing a shot. What did I have to lose? I saw some of my friends starting to quit their jobs to do this *thing* full-time too. If they could do it, I knew I could do it, so I went to work trying to build a business. I am forever grateful to that man Ray, who is now my husband!

Working for yourself sounds like a dream come true, and it's definitely worth it, but in the first five months I didn't make one sale or bring on one new person to my sales team. Needless to say I was discouraged. I had gone to all my broke friends and family to share my new business and ask them to support me and they all told me I was crazy. I was insulted. It was a huge blow to my ego unlike anything I had experienced before in life.

Frustrated and playing on my Facebook page, trying to make the time go by, I stumbled upon a story from a guy who had built his business using social media. I was intrigued. Once again I thought, "If he can do it, why can't I?"

Everything happens for a reason…

Facebook saved my business. Eighteen months after seeing that story and developing a strategy to grow my business online, I created a $10k per month income in the network marketing profession.

People from different companies were wondering what I was doing and were consistently asking me for the strategies I had been using to build my business to a six-figure per year income. It was then that I decided to create online training tools that people could use to build their home businesses via social media. Today both my networking business and my online coaching business are still going strong.

My husband and I now have a multiple seven-figure business between network marketing and our online training company, and we've been blessed to speak all over the world. I still pinch myself when I say this.

The moral of the story is: If a broke college student with no business experience and a tiny network can do it, so can you!

I mentioned I had a burning desire from the time I was little to be an entrepreneur. I realize that not everyone feels that way and that's OK! We all have unique gifts and we are going to show you how you can support your friends even if you don't want to open your own business. That's what makes the world work.

This book is for those who want to make a difference no matter where you fit in in the world.

I encourage you, if you have a desire to try something new, then pay attention to the opportunities and success stories we share in this book. They will help you take the first steps towards an amazing new chapter in your life. Then you'll know exactly what to do to create a life of freedom and you'll see how your passion and willingness to say 'YES' can make a difference in the world.

To get in touch with me and to sign up for free social media tips on how to grow your business, feel free to visit my website at www. JessicaHigdon.com. Now sit back, relax and enjoy the journey of *The Networking Revolution*. We're so glad you're here!

To Your Success,
Jessica Higdon

CHAPTER 1

The Many Faces of Home Business Ownership

*"Don't limit yourself. Many people limit themselves to what they think they can do.
You can go as far as your mind lets you. What you believe, remember, you can achieve."*

~ Mary Kay Ash

How did this book get into your hands? Was it given to you by a friend? Maybe you've been thinking about starting a home business or know someone who recently did? However this book materialized into your life at this moment, we welcome you and know you are in the right place at the right time.

Jessica and I are here for two basic reasons. First to challenge you to look deeper into the opportunities that home business ownership has to offer you today and secondly to suggest ways you can deliberately support your friends who have started their own home businesses.

Our approach is simple and we promise you'll learn something and have fun while you read!

Don't know if this is for you? Take a minute to check the following statements that are true for you and you'll see if what we have to offer makes sense for you now.

____ I would love to know how to earn extra money from home if it didn't interfere with what I'm currently doing.

____ Having a career or business that is flexible is important to me.

____ I am interested in finding a new way to use my professional skills and meet new people.

____ I have gotten caught up doing everything for everyone else and I would love to have something that was just mine.

____ I am an organized person who loves to work with systems and learns well from others.

____ I would love a little more recognition and praise in my life.

____ I have friends with home businesses and I want to understand what they're doing and see how I can support them.

Whether you want to escape the rigid hours of a traditional career, make some extra money or put a little bit of *you* back into your life, being your own boss can be very rewarding.

If you are like most women, there are things in your life that, given the right tools, opportunities or ideas, you'd change in a heartbeat. Maybe you'd like to know how to be home more with your children, work less hours at the bank or take an extra vacation. The ideas we share about home business ownership may get your creative juices flowing.

There are hundreds of opportunities available to women, like you, today to start a business from home for as little as $15, and hundreds of thousands of women who are making thousands of dollars a month doing it. We'll share some of their success stories a little later; let's not get ahead of ourselves.

You may be wondering why I am committed to help you understand your options and create a business and life you love. Let's talk about that.

Entrepreneurship Starts At Home

I grew up in a home where my father was an entrepreneur. At seventeen he started his first business teaching speedreading to top-level executives. Years later, after getting married and having my sister and me, he put himself back through school to get an MBA and became a CPA. He then returned to his entrepreneurial roots and opened his own accounting practice. He even taught himself computer programming and developed software on the side. That was pretty progressive back in the 1980s!

> *If you are like most women, there are things in your life that, given the right tools, opportunities or ideas, you'd change them in a heartbeat.*
>
>

It was fun going to his office on the weekends. He'd let me vacuum the carpet, empty the trash and wipe down the windows on the front door for a few dollars. I'd sit at the receptionist's desk and type on the electric typewriter. Being the first born, and a bit bossy, I knew that having my own business was the way to go.

My Entrepreneurial Beginnings

Six years into my journey as a stay-at-home mom of three girls I was beaten down. Although I had a degree in Elementary Education I had no interest in working with kids all day. In fact, I just wanted to get away from kids! That's the truth.

My husband supported me as an at-home mom. He was successful in his own business and was paying the bills but somewhere inside I felt like I wanted to have something of my own. What could I do? I had considered getting a waitressing job in the evenings to earn a little cash and get out of the house, but that didn't seem practical. I couldn't come up with any ideas that would not significantly alter my life as a mom until...

One routine day when I walked into our local dry cleaners and turned around to tell the kids to quiet down, I noticed a catalog that said "Start a Home Business for $15." My entrepreneurial light bulb flickered.

"Wow only $15? I can do that!" So I grabbed that catalog, stuffed it under my arm and headed home to make two phone calls. The first to the number on the catalog to inquire about the business and the second to my friend Rachel who came over and watched the kids so I could get started. I even borrowed the $15 from her because I had no cash on hand!

So thanks to a strategically placed catalog, a good friend and a little initiative, I was a business owner in a matter of hours. I had my own website, I had products I could sell and I had the flexibility to do it from home. This is the American dream.

"How did I do?" you ask.

Terrible.

The woman who helped me get started didn't train me. I didn't understand the business model. I was too scared to ask anyone else, but my family and friends, to buy from me. I had no sales skills or confidence. I didn't know there were local company meetings. In short, I had no idea how to run a business or that there was support available to me that I was not utilizing.

I ended up spending more money on my own samples, products and getting discounted 'demo' items as gifts than I ever did making money. For me, at that time, it was a great vehicle for discounted products and not so much a business. I eventually quit.

The Day of Reckoning

Fast forward a few more years. Still an at-home mom, I had completely lost myself in the to-dos of daily living. Everyone else's needs seemed to come first and the fun, carefree girl I used to be had withered into a crabby disillusioned woman. Who was this person?

In the quest to find myself again I made some bad choices that led me to a day of reckoning. I knew what I was doing with my life simply wasn't working and fortunately I was open to making some changes.

"How did I do?" you ask.

Thankfully, pretty well!

My family was supportive and I was smart enough to seek out a great therapist. I felt more confident in myself and the unhealthy guilt that caused my own misery began to dissipate. But what does that have to do with business?

Everything!

Your business is a reflection of you, so if you change yourself your business results will change too. Let's keep going and see how business number two started.

The Entrepreneur Emerges Again

The entrepreneurial spirit re-emerged as I regained my confidence. This time I wanted to help other women who were struggling in the same ways I had. If all it took was learning a few simple concepts like the importance of self-care then we could all be happy! My new mission was born.

Like many of us do when changing careers, I went back to school to become a Certified Life Coach and a year later opened up a private practice in Bonita Springs, FL. I had made it!

But where were the moms?

My clients ranged in age from twenty-four to seventy-three, both male and female. The majority were working women in their 40s-50s. I kept trying. My mentor, David Essel, said it takes 3-5 years to build a business and I needed to be patient. I hadn't given much thought to how hard it would be to start a business from scratch.

These women were enjoying all the benefits of business ownership without all the headaches I had experienced starting from scratch.

So I coached. And while I was being patient I also guest produced David's national iHeart Radio show and taught myself how to build websites. I learned how to blog, published a few books, learned how to record and edit videos, developed online courses and founded the University of Moms, which birthed two Happy Mom Conferences. And the money I made, I reinvested back into my business to keep it growing. I did this all while still being 100% mom.

Wow, owning a business was not what I thought it was as a child. It was exhausting! It took a very long time to build, a lot of skills to master and a lot of money. Years in fact and thousands of dollars!

Then in a flash of insight, the puzzle pieces of business ownership started fitting together inside my brain. There was an easier way to be a home-business owner and many women had already found it. Listen to this.

The Networking Revolution

A few months after my second moms conference I was casually going through the event photos. There were shots of the attendees having fun, shots of the speakers on stage and shots of the vendors selling their products. I slowed down.

Vendor by vendor I noticed a theme. Women in business. Women who were operating home-based franchises, aligned with a company they chose and selling products they loved.

This is called Direct Sales or Network Marketing. Super simple. Right? A textbook definition of direct sales is: "The direct personal presentation, demonstration, and sale of products and services to consumers, usually in their homes or at their jobs."

They saw what I saw years ago when I picked up that catalog, a way to earn extra income from home that was simple, affordable and flexible.

These women were enjoying all the benefits of business ownership without all the headaches I had experienced starting from scratch.

They were on teams, supporting each other, learning from each other and earning money together. Their website was done for them, the products and catalogs were first class and often the order fulfillment was handled remotely. Commissions were paid out from a corporate office and they had the opportunity to earn trips, attend conferences and advance up the leadership ladder at their own pace.

This is the networking revolution. It's the quickest, easiest and most affordable way to home business ownership there is in the world today. It's what we have termed, Franchising from Home (FFH), also known as Network Marketing or Direct Selling.

Note: For variety we will use these terms (FFH, Network Marketing and Direct Selling) equivalently throughout this book to refer to the opportunity to build a home-based business. Each company has its own nuances and compensation plans and we encourage you to do the research yourself if you choose to pursue any home business opportunity.

Franchising Versus Franchising From Home

We're all familiar with the concept of traditional franchising. My uncle owned a number of McDonald's franchises in Illinois years ago and my husband's fraternity brother owns a number of Moe's franchises here in southwest Florida. Buying a proven business system and getting the support of a larger well-established brand is a great model yet not very flexible or affordable for most.

If you have a few hundred thousand on hand you are a good candidate to start a traditional franchise. Some are a little less and some a LOT more. But you do have your options. Petty cash!

Don't have that kind of cash lying around? Then we have news for you. You can choose from hundreds of direct selling opportunities and align yourself with a company and product line you love and have your at-home business up and running in no time at all.

Guess what? Most FFH companies have a very low monthly overhead, if any. They provide you training and support and have a community of sales consultants who are working as much or little as they want to make their business fit in with their goals and lifestyle.

This is why so many women today are opting to replace their current income, or earn extra money in the nooks and crannies of their lives by opening a network marketing business. Read through the Home Business Matrix we have created for you now. We have showcased the similarities and differences between starting a business from scratch, opening a traditional franchise and opening a franchise from home. We encourage you to compare the various options available.

Although we know each column represents a model that is successful for some we feel the third represents the column that is the smartest choice for most women for many reasons, which you'll learn throughout this book. Please go to www.TheNetworkingRevolution. com to download your printable copy and share it with everyone you know. This is our way to help build awareness of the opportunities available to all of us today to be business owners and many still don't know they exist!

THE *Networking* REVOLUTION
HOME BUSINESS MATRIX

DIRECTIONS: What type of Home Business Opportunity is right for you? Take a minute to read through the three colored columns below. We believe that owning a home business is a great option for many women today and we hope our Home Business Matrix will help you see what category fits your desires, dreams and lifestyle best. Please feel free to print out as many copies as you'd like and share with other women who are considering opening a home-based business as well. Wishing you great success! *Jessica and April*

	Build Your Own Home Business	Open a Traditional Franchise	Franchise-From-Home (aka Direct Sales or Network Marketing)
Description	• Create your own service or product • Create the business systems to support it • Market and deliver your idea to your clients yourself Ex: Coaching/ Consulting Business	• Buy a franchise business system you can operate from home • Follow the training and deliver the service or product Ex: Bricks 4 Kidz, Tutor Doctor, Jazzercise	• Buy a franchise business system • Work your business from home • Follow the training and deliver the service or product (aka Direct Sales/Network Marketing) Ex: World Ventures, Isagenix, Thirty-One
How long to get it started	• Can take months sometimes years Depends on complexity and how quickly and aggressively you work and market your product or service.	• 6-8 weeks average This is from the time you sign the franchise agreement not including your time before you sign.	• Can take less than 24 hours Once you say "Yes" you can have a website and the ability to sell within a day or so. You can then start to earn as you learn.

The Networking Revolution ©2015 All Rights Reserved April O'Leary; Jessica Higdon

---

BONUS GIFTS: Earn 10K/Month on FB Training at JessicaHigdon.com and The Most Essential Ingredient to Building a Home Business at AprilOLeary.com.

	Build Your Own Home Business	**Open a Traditional Franchise**	**Franchise-From-Home** (aka Direct Sales or Network Marketing)
Initial Cost	• Plan at least $5,000 and re-investment as it grows Typically a product business has more up-front cost than a service business.	• Initial franchise fee is typically between $5K-$300K Fees vary. Consult your contract. See ongoing monthly overhead for more detail.	• Initial franchise fee is typically between $15 to $2,000 Fees vary. See ongoing monthly overhead for more detail.
What Does the Cost Cover	• You decide what you need to spend to get your business started. Ex: Website, marketing materials, logo, office space, outsourcing tasks, accounting, insurance, legal, etc.	• Your initial franchise fee is your ticket in the door. Every franchise is different with what is included in this fee. Tip: It's very important to read the details in your contractual agreement and consult a franchise lawyer before signing.	• Your initial franchise fee is your ticket in the door and you get your starter pack of products, website and company support. Tip: It's very important to access all the training provided. Your website and corporate support systems are included.
Monthly Overhead Cost	• Ongoing re-investment necessary, varies widely from a few hundred to thousands. This depends entirely on your business model and how aggressive or conservative you are. Plan on making mistakes along the way.	• Royalty fees are typically 4-6% of revenue. • Advertising fees also paid regularly. • Ongoing costs of operating a business. Again these fees are generalization and your contract will spell it out for you.	• Monthly minimum to remain active generally less than $100. • Ongoing costs of operating a business. Purchasing catalogs, samples or business cards are good investments.
Time Until Profitable	• Usually 3-5 years, could take longer. Knowing this will ground your expectations in reality. You have to stay the course and not quit.	• Varies widely based on franchise. You and your attorney will have to review the Franchise Disclosure Document (FDD) to see the statistics.	• Usually 30-60 days. Follow your company's fast-start program and you can earn back your initial fee and more in a very short period of time.

	Build Your Own Home Business	Open a Traditional Franchise	Franchise-From-Home (aka Direct Sales or Network Marketing)
Skills Required	• Positive Mental Attitude • Ability to create business systems • Financial • Technology and Social Media • Business Strategy and Planning • Lots more you'll learn along the way!	• Positive Mental Attitude • Ability to follow systems • Financial • Technology and Social Media • Business Strategy and Planning • Lots more you'll learn along the way!	• Positive Mental Attitude • Ability to follow systems • Financial • Technology and Social Media • Team Player • Lots more you'll learn along the way!
Support Received	• You are your own best cheerleader • Possible support from family or friends • Create mutually supportive business relationships	• Right to use franchisor's name/brand • Sources for equipment, signage purchases • Confidential operating manual • Initial training and grand opening support • Computer software • Ongoing support	• Right to use franchisor's name/brand • Trainig to help you fast-start your business • Sources for marketing materials • Company training and support • Grand opening support • Personal website and CRM • Ongoing support
Ability to Build a Sales Team	You can create an affiliate or referral program which you pay out based on sales generated.	You can hire sales people if necessary.	Team building a huge part of your business success. As you build your sales team you will earn a residual income based on your total.
Income Potential	• Entirely up to you! Your pay will be determined by how you structure your business and the revenue streams you create for yourself.	• Entirely up to you! Consult your Franchise Disclosure Document (FDD). The more franchises you open and run successfully the more money you'll make.	• Entirely up to you! Consult your Franchise Disclosure Document (FDD). The larger you are willing to build your sales team the more money you'll earn.

CONCLUSION: Which column seems the most appealing to you? Where can you go to learn more? Who do you need to talk with to get started? We aim to support you on the home business journey of your choice. To get your own digital copy of this form please download at TheNetworkingRevolution.com. We look forward to serving you!

Choosing Your Own Adventure

Whether you have already taken the leap into a home-based business or you are simply reading this because a friend shared it with you we promise you'll come away with some new information. We aren't here to make impossible promises or set unrealistic expectations. As with any business opportunity, you will get out of it what you put into it.

We hope that by the time you've finished reading this book, less than 60 minutes from now, you'll have:

1. A new respect for the women you know who have chosen to start their own home-based franchise

2. A willingness to shift your spending to support them and

3. Gained the knowledge and confidence to explore the idea of starting your own business from home.

This is truly a choose-your-own-adventure book. There are no right or wrong paths, it's up to you to decide what's right for you and we will help you navigate the way. Let's debunk some myths that you've probably already heard about this home-based business model.

Jess…you're on!

CHAPTER 2

Six Home Business Myths Uncovered

"The only good is knowledge, and the only evil is ignorance."

~ Socrates

Thanks, April, for sharing your personal story of entrepreneurship. In this chapter we'll break down commonly held myths about network marketing and in the following chapter I'll help you build back up your belief in the business model that has been helping people create financial freedom for over 150 years. Trust me when I say that in the past seven years I have seen countless women change their lives just from a simple shift in belief. It really can be that easy!

I mentioned in the introduction that when I first got started I failed for five months straight. I didn't sell a single product or bring on a single team mate. I had never owned my own business and I didn't understand what to do. That's enough to make anyone want to quit!

The good news is that I stuck with it and shifted my focus. I worked on building my belief in the networking profession. What that means is that I didn't totally understand that what I was doing would work. Yet somewhere inside of me I knew there was something to it. So I utilized the training that the company provided, I stayed consistent in my business building activities and I consciously maintained a positive attitude and I soon saw the results I was hoping for.

Assessing Your Current Beliefs

What's the first thing you think of when you hear the term *network marketing* or *direct sales*? Check the statements that you have heard before in association with this industry.

_____ It's a pyramid scheme.

_____ I've googled some of that before and it seems like a scam.

_____ I can get the products cheaper somewhere else, so why would I buy them from a friend?

_____ I don't like the feeling of my friends making money off of me.

_____ The people at the top make all the money. That's what I've heard.

_____ The only reason people get in it is to get rich quick. It never works.

If you checked any of the statements above, great! We are going to uncover the truth about these common myths in this chapter.

For now I want you to slow down and ask yourself:

1. Is my opinion about network marketing based on personal experience or was it derived from a family member, co-worker, or friend who had a negative experience?

2. If it was personal experience, was it the model of the business, the company or the products you had a problem with?

3. Was the person who introduced you to the opportunity unavailable to teach you so you didn't have great results?

Most of us don't initially choose our beliefs. We unconsciously embody what others believe until we take a minute to examine ours more closely and ask what is true for us.

I started out as a skeptic too. This is probably what led me to limited results the first five months of my home business journey. However, after opening my mind and choosing to learn more about this industry, I found the following to be true.

1. It has some of the best products on the market today.

2. It is probably one of the best business opportunities around.

3. It is an amazing vehicle to help people change their lives.

If you already have an existing FFH business, then this information will help you navigate some of the conversations that might have stumped you before. Education is the key and your ease in overcoming these myths will help countless other women experience the freedom, flexibility and financial success this model has to offer.

> *"The good thing about network marketing is anyone can do it, no matter your background or education. The bad thing is anyone can do it."*
>
>

It's so important to support the local women business owners you know to help keep them in business and to keep the economy strong. **In fact almost 80% of the direct sales industry is made up of women**. Let's get past these myths so we can start making this a win-win for everyone.

Common Myths about the Networking Industry

Below I've covered what I believe to be the six most common myths that are perpetuated about the networking industry and I have provided *myth-busters* to help you change your beliefs, if you dare.

Myth #1 – Network marketing is just a pyramid scheme.

This is probably the most common objection I hear from people who don't understand the business. Let's explore both the history of this term and why it is still used and the commission structure built into this type of business model.

When direct sales first hit the public market with the launch of Avon in 1886, the word for network marketing was called "pyramiding." It was called this because it was in the structure of a pyramid, much like any traditional business today.

Examine the hierarchy of a company like Apple and you'll see this same pyramid structure. The people at the top make more than the people at the bottom. Steve Jobs made a lot more money than an Apple store salesclerk and he had a lot more responsibility. Not too hard to see the logic in that.

Here is a general diagram of what it looks like out in corporate America today. Look closely. What shape do you see? Let's ask a few simple questions based on the image below.

In the corporate world:

1. What position(s) in a company generally earn the most money?

2. What position(s) earn the least?

3. How can a lower level employee make more money?

Pretty simple answers, right? Climb the pyramid. This pyramid structure is seen in almost all industries from education, to medicine, to politics and real estate. That's why people are always concerned with *climbing the corporate ladder.* The problem is that you need an invitation, a vote or a promotion from someone else to move up this ladder.

The good thing about direct sales is that you have the ability to promote yourself based on your own productivity. No invitation, schmoozing or promotion needed. Each company has laid out a leadership/compensation plan with achievable goals for you to follow.

Also, with no pressure from the company, you can choose your own adventure. You can build your business as large as you want as quickly as you want or maintain it as a hobby. You can succeed no matter what your background or education.

Although somewhere along the way the term "pyramiding" turned into "pyramid scheme," the model didn't change. It still creates millions of income opportunities for people around the world each and every year.

> *"The more you give the more you get. It's the law of reciprocity. Nowhere in that law does it state 'Only if they are the head of a major corporation or a non-family member or friend should you give.'"*
>
>

Fast Fact: There are over 5,000 network marketing and direct sales companies that fulfill all state and national regulations that any business would have to adhere to in order to operate and they have phenomenal products for consumers or else they would not be in business. Joining a direct selling company offers you a turnkey business with a very low start-up cost and provides all of the support and income opportunity of a traditional franchise.

The other 'pyramid scheme' objection revolves around the way money is made in this business model. There are typically two ways people who have a direct sales or network marketing business earn money.

First, they earn a commission based on the products or services they sell to their customers and second, they can earn additional team bonuses for helping other people who are interested to start a business.

You can see how this makes sense when you consider the value of time. Since this is a person-to-person business products are sold this way and new businesses are started this way as well. If a company did not pay you to help another person get started with their business then there would be little motivation to help train others. If there were little motivation to help others get started and share the business opportunity the company cannot grow. So each company has built in commissions and incentives so that you will be rewarded for spending your time helping someone else become successful.

Bottom line, when you are focused on helping your customers enjoy your products and you are helping develop others who are interested in the business you will be financially compensated for both.

We're going to highlight some women who are having great success in a dozen of these companies shortly and we encourage you to start searching for, purchasing from and encouraging your local direct sellers.

MYTH-BUSTER #1: If a company interests you, do your research. Remember to form your own opinions. The pyramid structure is commonplace in business and deciding to franchise from home is a very smart, low-risk and affordable way to start your own business. The huge benefit is that you get to choose how quickly you climb the ladder and there is a clear path laid out with specific instruction of what you must do to get there. No brown-nosing necessary!

Myth #2 – Google says bad things about it, so it must be true.

As long as the internet exists, there will be negative articles, scam videos, and generally miserable people with nothing better to do than bash new ideas, ambitious people and credible companies.

Google anything and you'll find someone somewhere with something bad to say. Have you spent any time on YouTube reading comments? Whoa! If you haven't look at any video and it won't take long before you find some nasty critiques. There are some crazy people out there!

Fast Fact: Anyone can post anything online and Google does not filter or monitor what is said for the most part.

Remember to always consider the credibility of the person offering their opinion and their motive. The good news is that you can form your own opinion based on facts.

Check out this video now by Ray. It is sure to give you a chuckle. http://rayhigdon.com/uh-oh-is-mlm-a-scam/.

MYTH-BUSTER #2: You can't please everyone all the time. Especially online! Yes, do your research. Yes, talk to a trusted friend. Yes, look at the company's track record. Finally, say YES if it is all looking good to you.

Myth #3 – I can get the product or service my friend is selling cheaper somewhere else.

Usually when people have this idea they don't realize they are comparing apples to oranges. If the products look the same but have completely different qualities or ingredients, it is not the same product. Buying shoes at discount retailer is not the same as buying shoes in a department store. Walk in them for a few hours and you'll soon see why there is a difference in pricing!

Fast Fact: Most networking companies have their own manufacturers, suppliers, doctors, chemists, proprietary and patented technologies, customer service support systems and more to make your experience first class. They are focused on creating only great products or services based on the mission of the company. This is why they are so successful.

Whenever I need laundry detergent, skincare, toiletries, vitamins, protein shakes, purses, travel, even legal services I always look for our local direct sales reps to see what they offer and often choose to buy from them.

And here's the kicker: a lot of times we pay even less than we would at those other retailers! Why not help a local entrepreneur, get better quality products AND save some money to boot? Seriously, that's a no-brainer.

Sometimes you may find products on the market of the same quality that you can get cheaper at those big stores, no question. That's when you weigh the pros and cons. Is it more important to you to save a couple bucks or to support a local entrepreneur who will be so grateful for your business? That's for you to decide.

Myth-Buster #3: When you consciously choose to buy from your local women entrepreneurs, you are not just supporting their businesses, you are supporting their lives, and that feels great. It ends up being mutually beneficial for both parties and supports the American Dream that we all love.

Myth #4 – It's not right for my friends to make money off of me.

This is one I understand better than anybody. Certain members of my family are so subconsciously conditioned to hate sales people that they will not buy a single thing from anyone in the family, no matter what they sell. In fact, they won't even get their hair cut by my cousin, who is a hairdresser, because they feel it's "not right" for her to make money off of family members.

Where would we be without sales in both our personal and professional lives? Salespeople provide a valuable service. When done well, salespeople help us get clear on what we need and then offer a product or service to help us solve our problem. If you've ever walked into a clothing store and been greeted by a gracious salesperson who showed you what was new, helped you incorporate some sales items and was attentive when you were in the dressing room you can appreciate sales.

As a parent you're constantly selling your kids on the idea that wearing a jacket when it's cold out makes sense and you're selling your spouse on the idea that going out to dinner makes more sense than cooking at home. So realize that sales is a part of being human. Whether you're selling purses or ideas, it's still sales!

Fast Fact: Understand that money is just an exchange for value– that's all. In the marketplace the more value someone provides, the more money they make.

If you or your friend have a product or service to sell that can help someone in some way, it is totally reasonable to ask for business from anyone who could benefit from it.

Myth-Buster #4: It's funny how simple it is. Supporting a friend's business would mean more to them than you realize and at the end of the day I promise you will feel good about helping them, too.

Myth #5 – The people at the top make all of the money.

I'm sure at some point you've heard that the people at the top "get lucky" and those are the only people that can make it big in this business. The fact of the matter is there are a ton of stories, mine included, that disprove this theory completely. If you out-perform the person above you, you can make more than them!

When I first got into network marketing, I entered at the bottom, just like everyone else. I wasn't given any special favors or given a "spot" at the top where all the leaders were. I also didn't get in super early. I got in after everyone I knew had already heard about it. For the first 6-8 months I was unknown in that company, until I started to put in the effort and treat it like a business.

Fast Fact: Ultimately I became the top female income earner in that company, was put on all the stages and was making more money than most people who "got in at the top." It had nothing to do with the structure, where I was placed or getting in early, it had everything to do with the effort I put in. The harder you work, the luckier you get it seems.

My friend Laura didn't come in at the top of her organization. In fact, she joined when the company was seven years old. They already had hundreds of thousands of consultants involved, but that didn't stop her from seeing the opportunity. Laura came in at the bottom like everyone else.

She now makes a solid six-figure income and loves the freedom she has created in her life. She can travel whenever she wants, take her kids to soccer games whenever she wants and pretty much do what she wants when she wants. You'll hear more success stories just like hers in Chapter 5.

Did she work hard to get there? Absolutely! And she would tell you that it was worth it. If she believed the myth "This is a seven-year-old company and there is no room for me to make it to the top—I'm going to pass..." her life would be very different.

The only people who make money are at the top is a myth that is simply untrue. Well, the only place that is absolutely true is in corporate America. Network marketing is a much more fluid business model where you are in control of your own success.

Myth-Buster #5: Working hard is more important than getting in early. Persistence is the only thing you need to succeed and you hold the keys to your own promotions. Even Lisa Wilber, an Avon representative featured in our Success Stories, has cumulative team earnings of over $4.5 million. She has created success for herself and she got in 100 years after Avon was founded!

Myth #6 – People are only in it to make money.

Making money is definitely a significant reason people join a networking company, no question. However, many people join for the top-notch business training and access to a community of successful people and others join for the perk of gaining access to discounts on amazing products they already love. In fact, 80% of people who join will focus on the non-monetary perks of being a part of a company.

First, let's talk about training and access to a community of successful people. In any other field you'd have to pay thousands upon thousands of dollars to gain access to top notch sales and business training and to successful people who are willing help you along the way.

But most networking companies provide sales training as part of your membership fee and most teams provide conference calls, Facebook support groups and live events to keep you engaged and inspired. Through these vehicles you'll meet a whole slew of new people who are positive and focused on making their lives successful.

Fast Fact: The benefit of the training alone is worth the initial fee. Whether you're super focused on your network marketing business, trying to start or grow a traditional business of your own, or you just want to improve yourself, the training you'll receive is first-class.

A good friend of mine owns a generator company and he also joined a networking company. Because of the training he's received through his affiliation with a networking company, and applying that knowledge to his traditional business, his generator company went from doing $100,000 in annual sales to over $400,000 in 12 short months.

"You mean for less than a thousand bucks I will have access to training that could skyrocket my primary business AND I would gain access to top producers as much as I want?" Yup! That's the power of this amazing model.

Second, when you become a member of a networking company you gain access to amazing products you already love at a discount.

Myth-Buster #6 – You know you have a great product when you have a lot of people purchasing and using your products because they love them and they continue to buy even though they are not interested in making money with the business. Having an active customer base is one key to building a solid business. Remember 80% of people love the perks and aren't interested in the business.

I cherish my loyal customers and I want as many product users as I can find. They bring excitement and credibility into my business and I love that they are happy simply from using my product (which is low maintenance on my end). They tell everyone how great it is too! Customers can be your best word of mouth advertising. I've actually found some of my best business builders through customers in my team.

If you see yourself as just a product user, that's fantastic. You'll see it come back to you in whatever venture you pursue in life.

Wrapping It Up

Pay attention to your reaction the next time you hear about an awesome new product in the direct sales profession or when your friend tells you she's opened a home-based business.

Check yourself. Do you immediately have negative thoughts? Do you shy away from it because you think the person selling it is just trying to 'get something' from you? You have to be very careful. If YOU have this thought process when being a consumer, you can't possibly convince other people to buy a product or service from you. You will be giving off this same negative energy in your sales interactions and others will feel like you are trying to 'get something' from them.

Subconsciously you'll sabotage your own success because of the underlying prejudice you have for sales people. My husband and I are the easiest people in the world to sell to. We'll buy anything we see value in. That's because we know it'll come back to us. We act in the world how we would want our ideal customer to act and it's been a blessing to see it come full circle.

Now that we've broken down the six biggest myths in the networking industry today, let's build back up our belief with statistics and success stories that are sure to wow you into action.

CHAPTER 3

Fast Facts and Celebrity Endorsements

*"The richest people in the world build networks.
Everyone else looks for work."*

~ Robert Kiyosaki

Now that you're aware of the common "myths" of franchising from home, let's dive into some hard statistics that you may not know about our industry.

There are several ways you can use the information in this chapter, and really in this entire book. First, use these stats to help support your own belief in the power of network marketing. Second, use them to help educate others who might not understand or who may have misinformation.

The more awareness and positive energy we can create together, the more everyone wins. Now before we take a look at the statistics, let's take a look at some of the problems we're facing as a society.

The Complex Problem We're Facing

We are all aware that both the global and U.S. economies are shifting. Even with the spike in real estate, lower oil prices and the economic boom, we are still closing in on $18 trillion in debt and by 2019 are projected to reach almost $21 trillion. The growing economy at this rate cannot likely be sustained with these numbers.

Some suspect that Social Security is on its way out, since the U.S. government is losing almost $80 billion per month, and people are realizing that the only person they can count on for retirement is themselves.

> *"The richest people in the world build networks. Everyone else looks for work."*
> *~ Robert Kiyosaki*

Not only are retirees suffering from this economic issue, but students are also facing tough times. According to the Huffington Post:

"To give you some context, 40 million Americans now have at least one outstanding student loan, with the average borrower carrying four different education-related loans. These numbers have pushed the student debt crisis to epic proportions, setting the amount of collectively-held student debt at an all-time high of $1.5 trillion.

This crisis has also given rise to a generation of "boomerang kids," with legions of college graduates putting off moving out, starting a family and buying a home due to overwhelming student debt. The average class of 2014 graduate left college $34,000 in the hole."

The DailyCaller.com cites that approximately just 14 percent of college graduates are finding jobs. This is putting many on the slow track to success and is causing a significant generational spending gap. The less successful the next generation, the less consumerism exists and the more our economy suffers.

On top of that, because of our country's debt we are becoming more rigid with government grants for scholarships. I don't foresee this problem going away, and I believe the best solution is taking responsibility for your own life and finding a way to create financial independence despite these grim statistics.

Now let's take a look at how direct selling offers a simple solution. Warning! These facts may shock you and you may question if they're real! I can assure you that every statistic you're about to see is accurate and backed by some of the largest organizations in our country including the Direct Selling Association.

Fast Facts about Network Marketing and Direct Sales

According to CNN Money in 2014 the total revenues for the NFL were $12 billion. Pretty impressive. Right? Looking further into statistics from Statista.com are the global stats of the music industry at $15 billion, the video game industry at $46.5 billion.

However, beating these out by a long shot is the network marketing industry which sold $167 billion in products worldwide, $34 billion of that business was conducted in the U.S. and the industry paid out over $65 billion in commissions globally. Those are some pretty solid numbers and I am proud to be professionally associated with one of the largest industries in the world!

Here are some quick statistics about the state of the network marketing industry in the U.S., according to the Direct Selling Association as of 2014. All of these can be found directly on their website www.dsa. org and you can of course go digging for even more than what we've given you here.

- 18.2 million people in the U.S. are involved in direct selling
- 74.4% of those involved are women
- 76% of sellers have been with their company 1+ years
- 78% of sellers say direct selling meets or exceeds their expectations
- 82% of sellers report a good, very good or excellent experience with direct selling
- 74% of US adults have purchased products from a direct seller
- 71% of sales are person-to-person, 22.4% of sales are by parties and 6.1% other sales

- $34.47 billion sales in total U.S. sales annually

What's also interesting is that if we look over time there is no significant decrease in sales, only steady growth, no matter what type of economy. People are craving a chance to be their own boss and build a business that includes residual income. Many are realizing that plan B isn't working any more or simply want more flexibility in the ways they choose to make money.

As you can see, Direct Selling is one of the leading channels people purchase products and services through. There is no doubt that the concept works and is gaining momentum each and every year.

Powerful People Endorsing Network Marketing

Robert Kiyosaki, one of the top real estate moguls in the world and the author of *Rich Dad, Poor Dad,* often says that network marketing and direct sales are two of the lowest risk ways to become wealthy.

You might find it interesting that BusinessForHome.org showcases some other big names that endorse the industry like Madeline Albright, Jim Rohn and even President Bill Clinton who shows his support back in 1996 in this short video clip at www.apriloleary.com/clinton.

Richard Branson and Warren Buffett are also known for being avid consumers of the direct sales industry, and in fact, own a majority of shares in several direct sales companies.

Branson, founder of the Virgin brand, has a significant stock portfolio in a cosmetics company called *Virgin Vie at Home* and Buffett, notorious billionaire and one of the richest men in the world, owned a direct sales company called *The Pampered Chef.*

Here's what Buffet had to say about it:

"We are extremely excited about *The Pampered Chef.* Doris Christopher has created from scratch an absolutely wonderful business."

Suzanne Sproul, reporter for the Inland Valley Daily Bulletin, says in her article *"From Tupperware Parties to Purse Parties, Party-Plan Marketing Making a Comeback,"*

that because of the impersonal aspect of technology in our society today, people are starting to crave a fun, in-person atmosphere to buy their products. Even those without a need for a side income are excited to buy from a local entrepreneur.

You'd think with technology and the ease of buying online, direct sales would be fading but the person-to-person interaction, combined with the convenience of direct shipping, has helped sales increase steadily each month.

She writes:

"The depth and breadth of products one can buy while sitting on the living room couch with a few friends is virtually limitless. More than six decades after the first

"...40 million Americans now have at least one outstanding student loan, with the average borrower carrying four different education-related loans. These numbers have pushed the student debt crisis to epic proportions, setting the amount of collectively-held student debt at an all-time high of $1.5 trillion..."
~ Huffington Post

Tupperware party, people are now hosting parties where guests can check out products from personal self-defense items (Damsel in Defense) and tea collections (Zendigo Teas) to nail polish (Jamberry Nails) and pet products (pawTree). In a time when technology can seem overwhelming to many, the personal touch of the home party is not only fun, but fills a need for personal selling and customer service."

Why are some of the smartest and richest men and women in the world starting to invest their hard-earned money into these companies? They believe in the power of person-to-person sales, they value the idea of helping others succeed and they see the potential for growth that this industry offers.

Powerful Global Statistics

Not only has the network marketing community taken the U.S. by storm, but it is also making a huge impact globally. Look at the countries who are huge players in this industry like China, Japan, Korea and Brazil.

Global Direct Selling – 2014 Retail Sales

Published May 29, 2015

Not for use after May 28, 2016

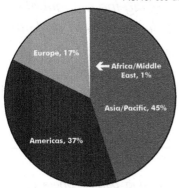

Regional Sales

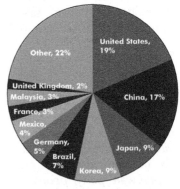

Top 10 Global Markets

Global Industry: $182,823 (USD millions), Up 6.4% in Constant 2014 USD

The numbers don't lie. Direct sales brought in over $182,823,000,000 globally (that's $182 billion) in 2014 and their numbers are continuing to rise into 2015.

The more shocking number in my opinion is that there are almost 100 million direct sellers in total! This proves that there is certainly no shortage of entrepreneurs to purchase from, no matter where you live.

The Simple Solution

The economic problems our society and world are facing are complex, yet the solution on an individual level can be simple. I believe that the opportunity available for business ownership through network marketing and direct sales partly solves this economic problem in several ways:

First, you have a low risk, high-income potential opportunity to get back on your feet. You control your income based on how hard you work and you can set yourself up with a nice residual income for retirement.

In fact, researchers say that an extra $500 per month would prevent most foreclosures in the United States! With a simple marketing you can easily create an extra $500 a month on a part-time basis. This one step puts money back into your pocket and back into the markets. The more fortunate our population, the more they can give back to society and increase consumerism.

Second, as a consumer of direct sales products and services you play a huge role in helping keep the economy strong. By circulating money back into the hands of entrepreneurs you're bridging the gap between the big box stores who hold a majority of the market, and the mom and pops or local direct sellers who are trying to support themselves. This shift in spending plays a vital role in our economy's health and in your future, no matter who you are or what you do.

I hope that now you understand the huge impact the network marketing industry has on personal success and the global economy.

You have seen the statistics and people who support it, and we hope you will make a commitment to get involved in some way--either as a consumer, a hobbyist, or even an entrepreneur. Let's talk about the varying ways you can get involved. I'll turn it back over to you, April.

CHAPTER 4

Five Ways Women Are Changing Their Lives

"Women have always been the strong ones of the world."

~ Coco Chanel

The Networking Revolution is here. It is ready and waiting for you to jump in feet first at whatever level of involvement you decide is right for you. In this chapter we'll discuss five different ways you can say 'yes' to being a part of an industry that involves over 18 million people in the U.S. and millions more world-wide.

Are you open? Your answer to this one question will reveal a lot about you. Being open simply means that you're able to listen to new ideas without judgement. Being open means you are aware that you have more to learn. **Being open is a state of mind that is growth-oriented.**

What's the alternative? Being closed. I'm sure you've met people like that! They say 'no' to new ideas and opportunities. They have their own already-formulated opinions about a lot of things and they often get stuck. They are rigid and I know you don't want to be that!

Let's agree to be open as we browse through the five options presented below. Carefully consider each one and see where you fit in right now. Remember that saying 'yes' to any option is a great point of entry. There is no right or wrong choice here. Simply find what is best for you and know that you can change your answer at any point in the future and in fact many do.

Check the box below each section that sounds like an option you would consider.

Option 1: Consumer

"I am willing to shift my spending from big box stores to women entrepreneurs whenever logical and possible. I will actively seek out and collect their information to purchase from them in person or online."

Did you know that for every $100 spent at a local business, $68 goes back to the community? This entry point is easy. Everyone can say 'yes' to this level of involvement. What does that mean? Being a consumer in The Networking Revolution simply means you are willing to shift your spending from big box stores to supporting direct selling associates whenever logical and possible.

This is where the resource section of the book will come in handy. Your job is to be a scout. You are actively looking for and collecting information from women who own their own businesses. Then the next time you need something that they sell, you call them or order from their online store rather than driving to your local chain store.

____ YES I am willing to actively shift my spending to support my home business friends. I now understand how important it is to purchase locally so that my money can stay in my community.

Option 2: Supporter

"I am willing to actively refer business to a women entrepreneur. I will consider hosting a party for my local representative or making introductions whenever possible. I want to see my friend succeed!"

Being a supporter is just that. You are supportive. You are not quite ready to pay a member fee to be an associate but you are cheering your friend on 110% and are willing to help them build their client base. This is what being a supporter is all about.

A "Supporter" is the person who knows when they help someone else reach their goals, they end up getting it back tenfold. I have an awesome hair dresser named Jennifer and I could just go and leave it at that. But she is amazing! You can bet I send people her way when they ask me where I get my hair done. Being a supporter is absolutely the same thing!

How to Support a Direct Selling Business Friend

Instead of just buying products, you offer to host a party for your friend. It's easy to do. Over the years I've hosted parties for my friends who have businesses with Thirty-One, Tastefully Simple, Pampered Chef and Stella and Dot. It's a great excuse for a girl's night out and means more to them than you probably ever imagined.

A Story from Jessica: *The other day I went to an Essential Oil party. I don't sell oils nor do I have any connection to the person who was selling the oils. However my friend, Kirsten, invited me and had been telling me how great the product had been for her newborn. My friend didn't sell the oils either. She just loved the product so much she decided to host a get together to promote them for her friend, Megan. I went to hear the information with the intention of becoming a product user, and the rest is history.*

I bought a bunch of product, which benefited my friend Kirsten (who got some free products for hosting) and Megan of course. The best part is I got to meet and really connect with Megan (the essential oils rep). Because I train network marketers on building their businesses online, she decided to attend our major event, Top Earner Academy, and purchase my Social Media Local Prospecting Formula (www.SocialMediaLocalFormula.com).

We are now friends and customers of each other. Had my friend Kirsten not hosted that essential oils party, Megan and I would have never met and we would have never done business together. Everything comes full circle.

Match-Making Business-Style

I do a lot of business match-making each week. My mind is always thinking about how I can introduce people I know who can do business together. This is what being a supporter is all about. It's taking a more pro-active role in helping.

Your home-business friends have one of two business models. They are either building through a party business (direct selling) or they are building a business through one-to-one business meetings (network marketing). The best way to help your friend with this type of business is to introduce them to people you already know. This role is what Malcom Gladwell calls the 'Connector' in his book *The Tipping Point*. This is a very important role in society and it's the way you can help someone's business grow from being mildly successful to wildly successful.

Here are a few easy ways to do this.

1. Ask your friend what type of client they are seeking. Do they need introductions to gym owners, doctors, personal trainers, mom groups or other business leaders?

2. Go through your phone, email and/or social media contacts and see who you know that fits their profile. You may come up with a few ideas on your own, too.

3. Contact those people and get permission to make an introduction. Unless you know that there is a mutually beneficial business relationship that can develop, it's always customary to ask permission before handing over a contact.

4. Make the introduction.

Here are a few of the ways I successfully make introductions every week.

In-Person Introduction – If you live in the same area, this is the best way to make an introduction. Contact each person and invite them to

THE Networking REVOLUTION

a coffee where you will make the introductions. Make sure you set up the expectations before the meeting.

Here is a sample script:

"Hi Sarah and Claire! I have known you both for a while and think you two would love to meet. Sarah has a nutritional cleansing business and I love the results I'm getting using her products. Claire, I know how you love trying new health products too. I thought you might enjoy hearing more about it. Sarah, Claire is an amazing person, a mom of three and teacher at our school. She's a real asset there! Want to all meet up at The Coffee Bean on Thursday evening?"

Email Introduction – If you don't live in the same area, or scheduling is not conducive to an in-person meeting, then an email introduction works well. You can also do this on Facebook as a joint Direct Message.

Here is how that could work:

"Hi Sarah and Claire! I was thinking of you two recently and know you two have a lot in common. Sarah has a nutritional cleansing business and I'm loving the results I'm getting. I'm down 5 lbs. already! Claire, I know how you love trying new health products and thought you might enjoying chatting or scheduling a phone call to learn more. Sarah, Claire is a mom of three and a teacher at our school. She's such an asset! I'm happy to get on a 3-way call. Would next Tuesday after dinner work? I hope this is helpful! Thanks for being great friends!"

Both direct sellers and network marketers would fall over backwards for your support and referrals. In fact, learning to make strategic introductions is a skill anyone can learn and can help people move their businesses forward more quickly. It's match-making business-style. Make a point to introduce people you know to those who can help them.

____ YES I am willing to connect people I know for the mutual benefit of both. I will host parties when asked or send referrals to support my home business friends. Who can I call now to book a party? Who can I refer to a friend? Hmm…let me think!

Option 3: Member

"I know a deal when I see it. I want to join this company and enjoy the perks of membership.

I am not sure I want to be a part of the business yet but I definitely want my own account and am willing to learn more about the culture and community of the company."

> *Being open is a state of mind that is growth oriented.*
>
>

About 80% of any company is made up of a consumer base of members who simply love the products and decide they want the benefit of being able to purchase those products at discounted pricing. Being a member also means you open yourself up to the opportunity to start making money if you so choose.

If this is you, great! We need you. Being a member is just the same as joining your local wholesales store or gym. You will pay an annual or monthly membership fee to be able to shop at discounted pricing. Additionally, you will gain a sense of community because you now have access to all of the company training and events which you can choose to attend if you want.

Most companies have annual conventions and smaller weekend training events throughout the year which can enhance your life both personally and professionally. All members are invited if they are at this level or higher. There are people I know who are members of companies just for the event and community benefits.

In fact, as I mentioned in Chapter 1 for six years I was a member of a skincare company. I loved ordering their demo jewelry at a steeply discounted pricing. I bought presents for friends and family through my membership and had a few customers ordering from my online store. For me, at that time, it was perfect.

Many women who start out as members soon find that they love the company and the products so much that it is natural to start sharing. If this is the case they graduate up into the next category of Hobbyist.

_____ YES there are products I would love to be able to purchase at discounted pricing. I would certainly consider joining a company as a member for that reason. Heck, I might even enjoy going to the company's motivational event with some new friends, too!

Option 4: Hobbyist

"I would love to open an account and learn how to get my products for free. Who wouldn't? You know what…earning an extra $500-$1000/ month sounds pretty good to me right now."

For many women becoming a hobbyist comes quite by surprise. Maybe you attended a party, enjoyed the evening and bought some products. Then after looking further at the catalog you decided you wanted to join as a member to get discounted pricing. You hang out at that level and realize the person that helped you sign up is super supportive and they're making extra money too. You're intrigued.

This is a huge benefit of being in the industry. When you join as a member you become part of a family of successful people who want to help you. Your team leader may give you a new member survey to see what your goals are with your business. You may not know exactly but the idea of getting products free and earning some 'fun money' seems doable and you know it could help your family in a lot of ways.

So you take a few small action steps. You start learning from the training provided. You get the courage up to talk to a few friends and family and suddenly you find you're making some money with just a part-time effort.

Here is the secret. You just have to be coachable and follow the formula from those who are already successful in your company. Can you do that? Learn and follow directions? I'm sure you can. This is what's so great about this type of home business. You don't have to guess as you go like I did when I opened my coaching practice back in 2010.

Opening a business with a direct sales company is just like opening any other franchise. You get the support, the training, the systems, the website and more…all for a ridiculously low start-up fee. This is what's so exciting. To start a business with most companies will cost less than $500 and they will teach you how to earn that money back in less than 30 days.

Ask your friend who helped you get started as a member how you can earn your money back and start getting your products for free. They would LOVE to help you!

_____ YES I would love to learn how to earn an extra $500 or more a month. I am willing to learn from others and can follow systems as they are taught to me. This sounds exciting!

Option 5: Entrepreneur

"I had no idea! You mean I can make more money in this business than I do at my current job AND I can set my own hours and work from home? I'm in!"

The word entrepreneur is one you might not have thought of to describe yourself before. I mean look at Entrepreneur magazine and you'll see young guys living in Silicon Valley creating the next giant tech company and seeking investors for millions of dollars. Yet, the definition of an entrepreneur is *a person who organizes and operates a business or businesses, taking on greater than normal financial risks in order to do so.*

Here's what is great! In this industry you *do not* have to take on greater than normal financial risks in order to be successful. As I've mentioned, most of the time you can earn back your initial investment before your credit card statement arrives in your mailbox. You simply have to follow the systems laid out for you and work them every day. The quicker you work and the more you learn, the more successful you'll be.

This is what being an entrepreneur really means to me. It means you are willing to work hard and you understand that your success is 100% reliant on you. There is no paycheck that will show up on Friday without your effort. However, with your effort the sky is the limit. There is no cap on your income. There is no scheduled raise every year that deadens your desire to work harder because no matter what you do, you will never earn more than the Excel spreadsheet has laid out for your position.

See that? It's exciting!

So if you're even just a little curious, even if you're just a little competitive, even if you're just wondering what you're made of and you're up for a challenge that your current career is not offering you, this just may be the right choice.

In this option there are two categories we have identified as Entrepreneurs. They are the Accidental Entrepreneur and the Intentional Entrepreneur and you could be either! Let's see what you think.

The Accidental Entrepreneur

Sounds funny, right? But this is like a lot of life's happenings. How did you get into your current career? How did you meet your spouse? How did you learn how to build a website? Maybe it's just me, but a lot of my life has been somewhat accidental, or shall I say serendipitous.

When I say 'accidental' I don't mean bad. What I mean is what happened isn't what I thought would happen. I became a mom at the ripe old age of 24. That was a huge blessing but not exactly intentional. I became a life coach (intentional) but then taught myself how to build websites and write books, create online courses and put on conferences. That was accidental.

You see when I set out to get my coaching certification I thought I'd be coaching moms in an office. Today I mainly coach business owners in my private practice and it is now done by Skype, phone and email.

Think about where you are right now. How did you get there? Did you have the full vision and you checked off one item at a time or was it somewhat more organic than that?

You may not have a clear end result. You might not know how to get there. Yet you might see the possibility as real and you're smart enough to know that if someone else can do it, you can do it too, but maybe you're not ready to commit full-time to a new business yet. That's fine.

You can start like Lindsey Catarino who built her Beachbody business alongside of her full-time job in banking. She accidentally got into the business after using the workout program herself before her wedding and subsequently sharing her pictures on Facebook. Everyone noticed how amazing she looked and asked her what she was doing!

This led her to a crossroads. She decided to keep a list of interested people on her desk and reach out to a few per day with the limited time she had. Just 16 months later she had replaced her banking income and was faced with another crossroads. Should she keep building her Beachbody business or accept a Vice President position the bank had just offered? Needless to say, she recognized the opportunity she had in front of her and knew, if it didn't work out, she could always go back to banking.

What a great decision! Now, just three years into her business she is on track to make a million dollars in commissions. I recently interviewed her on Network Marketing TV and I invite you to hear what she has to say about her journey as an Accidental Entrepreneur at http://bit.ly/lindseycatarino.

You, too, might see the possibilities and if you are willing to commit 5-10 hours a week working a 'side business,' you never know what might come of it. Maybe you will end up building a large business just like Lindsey did.

_____ YES I can see the potential in building a business like this and I'd love to start building and see where it takes me.

The Intentional Entrepreneur

"I want to be on page 8 of the catalog."
Cherie Rodriguez,
Thirty-One Gifts, Independent National Executive Director

I met Cherie over a year ago before my second Happy Mom Conference. We hit it off like long lost sisters and I invited her to speak to the women who attended about her own journey to making money with meaning.

> *Being an entrepreneur means you are willing to work hard and you understand that your success is 100% reliant on you.*
>
> ∞

Being a former teacher-turned-stay-at-home mom, she was lost in her life of family duties. A common story for many of us, to be sure. After being invited to a Thirty-One party, cancelling last minute and eventually placing an outside order, she was prodded by a close friend to join the company with her. She did.

Sitting in her car, scared before her first vendor event, she made her way inside and set up her table. That afternoon changed her life. Woman after woman was asking about the bags she was selling and she left with a confidence that she could grow a business. Now six years later she has reached the top level of her company and is not slowing down anytime soon.

Jessica had a similar experience. She mentioned in her intro that she was searching for something to change her current situation. She was overworked, broke and had no time freedom.

At that time she was skeptical of network marketing. She heard, much like the myths we busted earlier, that it was a pyramid and a lot of other ignorant thinking. Luckily she had a thick skin and after educating herself, she knew it was the perfect vehicle for her to change her circumstances. That doesn't mean she became successful overnight. It does mean she caught the vision for 'what could be' and worked hard to hone her skills and build her business.

The intentional entrepreneur is very goal oriented and has a desired outcome. They often get to that full time income status much quicker than the accidental entrepreneur because they start with clear intentions and the focused energy needed to build a big business from the very beginning.

You may fall into this category if you have the following characteristics:

- **Coachable** – You are willing to follow a system and don't have to do everything "your own way."

- **Burning desire to help others** – Extremely strong reason and motivation to own your own business.

- **Fed up with current circumstances** – Maybe you're in a toxic relationship, maybe you're tired of not taking family vacations, maybe you'd like to get out of debt or break-free from a rigid career schedule…whatever your reason, building a home-business can help you change your life!

- **Ready to make sacrifices** – Being an entrepreneur (especially in the beginning stages) means you may have to sacrifice some quality time with the family, movie nights, date nights, negative relationships, etc. Understand that it is only temporary (12-36 months).

SIDE NOTE: Make sure to talk with your family about WHY you're making these sacrifices. Sit them down and have a heart to heart. Listen to their concerns and be reassuring that you have a time frame in mind to create this success you are sharing with them. They will respect you for it. Make sense?

- **OK With Rejection** – As the saying goes: *People's opinions don't pay your bills.* In any business, you have to be able to handle rejection. Remember that who you are on the inside can never be shaken by what happens on the outside. Read that again. Your worth is never determined by what others think of you. Having a business is a great way to prove that to yourself!

If you have all of the above characteristics and you are still scared to take the leap, do it anyways. Every single successful person on planet earth still has fears and doubts. There are no guarantees. The difference is they take a chance on themselves.

We understand the challenges that come with not knowing anything about building a business. We didn't know how to build one either but we started and chose to learn along the way.

Don't know where to get your leads from, or even how to sell? That's ok, you'll learn. Jessica went from not knowing anything about being a business owner to building a multiple seven-figure empire in a few short years, and if she can do it, you can too.

In this business you are never alone—which is another reason it's perfect for women. By nature most women are social and learn best from others. You'll have plenty of teammates and more training than you could possibly want. There are countless books on business building and if you have extra money to invest in yourself, you can always hire a business coach or purchase some online training to improve your skill set.

Most professionals are required to submit continuing education credits or certifications to keep their licenses up to date, so make sure you reinvest in yourself too. Once you have some income coming in, it's important to allocate some time and money to sharpen your skill set and commit to learning more on a regular basis. This success of your business is highly dependent on your own level of self-awareness and your commitment to personal growth.

Treat this business as a hobby, and you will earn a hobby income. Treat this business as your empire, and you will create an empire-sized income. It's your choice.

_____ YES I am ready to see my face in my company's catalog. If Cherie and Jessica can do it so can I. Now let me get busy finding the right company to join.

It's time to decide. Which category best describes you? Look back through the chapter and check the YES statement that resonates most with you at this moment in time.

I'm excited that we've helped you start the journey with the right expectations. This is where it starts to get fun. **Being an entrepreneur means you are willing to work hard and you understand that your success is 100% reliant on you**.

Whether you decide to be a consumer, a supporter, a member, a hobbyist or an entrepreneur you will have chosen to change your life and the lives of those involved in home businesses for the better.

We've compiled a number of success stories of women from various companies who are changing their lives and helping countless others too. The one common thread you'll find is they are all regular women, just like us, who made something really great happen through a decision to do something different, a commitment to learn and a vision to succeed.

Let's keep going and see what they have to share with us.

CHAPTER 5

14 Home Business Success Stories

"If you don't go after what you want, you'll never have it. If you don't ask, the answer is always no. If you don't step forward you're always in the same place."

~ Nora Roberts

You may have read this far and thought, "Ok, so I know April and Jessica have seen success, but is it really true that anyone can do this type of business? Who else is seeing results?"

There have been thousands of women who have created financial freedom beyond what they ever conceived. It is possible for anyone from any background to create that success.

We have asked some of our friends and leaders in the industry to share their stories with you. We are so grateful for their time and hope their experiences will encourage and inspire you to take action today.

It may take some time, but it is important to us that you understand the enormous shift in thinking you'll undergo. In a traditional career you often trade time for money. When you choose to own a business you are going to work your face off in the beginning often with little to show for it. Don't let that discourage you. The pay-off is worth it in the end. When you build a sales team you are creating a residual income where you are paid on your own efforts AND on the efforts of everyone on the team. This is the power of residual income.

Remember the stories we are sharing are of women just like you. They are at-home-moms, teachers, government workers, stock traders, realtors, physical therapists and waitresses. Pay attention their varied backgrounds and feel free to highlight someone of interest or jot down their story. It may come in handy to remember them when you need some motivation for your day.

Note: The companies represented in these stories are just a sampling of many reputable companies available in the network marketing industry today and there was no specific strategy to select them over another company other than we knew these women personally. Please understand there is no way we could include every company or this book would be the size of Texas. So if your company is not represented, know that we still support and value your efforts to build a life of freedom in the company of your choosing and we encourage you to see this as a representative sample of ALL companies and what is possible for anyone to achieve.

For the sake of brevity we chosen to share these fourteen success stories in an abbreviated format that we believe will be easy to read. Much of what is written has been left in the original words of the person who is speaking directly to you. We did this for authenticity. We encourage you to make an effort to reach out to them on Facebook, ask them more about their journey and tell them how their story has impacted you. Nothing would mean more to them!

If you have a heart of service, and you are inspired and driven by helping others, this is the right business to be in!

Without further ado, let's hear from our amazing panel of networking rock stars!

NAME: Lora Ulrich

YEAR STARTED NETWORK MARKETING: 2001

PROFESSIONAL BACKGROUND: Engineering Assistant & Alaska Department of Labor Employment Specialist, Nutrition and Weight Loss Coach

COMPANY: USANA

JOINED CURRENT COMPANY: 2001

HOW DID YOU FIND OUT ABOUT YOUR COMPANY?: A good friend approached me when I came back from vacation. I thought she had lost her mind or been abducted by aliens!

SUCCESS STORY: Because I was trying to save my friend from Network Marketing (silly me), I did some serious research and ended up joining instead! I have now spoken in front of 10,000 people, won three awards in rank advancement, and in 2012 I was 29th in the company for growth in income. It has been awesome! I loved being on stage at our annual company event and having team members on stage with me. The support I received from everyone was amazing. My husband, step-daughter and 6-month-old granddaughter were there, which made it even better. Because of our residual income we were able to move from Alaska to warm Florida weather, yay!

> *Remember these are women just like you.*
>
>

WORDS OF ADVICE: Follow your heart. Don't listen to naysayers. Be teachable and never give up!

Lora now has a team of thousands and went from trading time for money with her health and wellness consulting, to becoming totally free. It's funny how she was trying to save her friend and in the process she saved herself. Congratulations on all your success Lora. We're so inspired by you!

NAME: Danielle Russo-Slugh

YEAR STARTED NETWORK MARKETING: 2008

PROFESSIONAL BACKGROUND: Wall Street Sales Trader, owned and operated a Broker Deal off the Trading Floor of the New York Stock Exchange

COMPANY: Isagenix

JOINED CURRENT COMPANY: 2011

HOW DID YOU FIND OUT ABOUT YOUR COMPANY?: A friend showed it to me when my husband, Marc, was battling stage four Hodgkin's lymphoma and suggested we use the products to help rebuild his body. We loved the products and company so much it just made sense to jump in and share the products with our friends and family.

SUCCESS STORY: In trading you only earn income 6.5 hours a day from 9:30 a.m., when the bell rings, until the bell rings again closing business at 4:00 p.m. In my current business it's truly a miracle to earn income 24/7/365 and not have to trade time for money anymore. Marc is now 2.5 years in remission and in the best shape of his life—boxing, lifting, surfing, and being a healthy dad to our 5 kids. I just completed my first Sprint Triathlon and am an avid cross-fitter, kickboxer and yogi. Leading by example with a healthy happy life and kicking cancer in the butt has been an incredible journey for us and we are grateful for the vehicle of Isagenix and the industry of network marketing.

WORDS OF ADVICE: Are willing to be internally motivated? Are open to coaching? Are you ready to look in the mirror and commit to some serious personal growth? Do you have a heart of service, and are you inspired by helping others? If you answered YES to those questions then the sky is the limit!

Even though her job was a very high paying job, she still didn't have the one thing we all strive for, freedom. Over the past three and a half years Danielle has built a team of 5,000 people with very little networking experience. She has now moved to Florida and works on her own terms. Thank you Danielle for generously sharing your story and for helping so many others live healthier lives and experience financial freedom through your business! Way to go!

NAME: Beth Leipold

YEAR STARTED IN NETWORK MARKETING: 2006

PROFESSIONAL BACKGROUND:
Physical Therapist Assistant, Personal Trainer and Fitness Instructor

COMPANY: Juice Plus+

JOINED CURRENT COMPANY:
2006

HOW DID YOU FIND OUT ABOUT YOUR COMPANY?: Two friends who attended a Juice Plus+ presentation came up to me after a fitness class I was teaching to ask me about it. They were not in the business and wanted to know if I had heard of it and if I had any

> *Beth went from being in foreclosure and her confidence totally shattered to becoming a superstar and inspiration in her company.*
>
>

opinions. I had never heard of Juice Plus+ at that time so I was curious to learn more about it.

SUCCESS STORY: My husband and I were on the brink of foreclosure on a house and possible bankruptcy. Once I decided to build a Juice Plus+ business things started to change and my biggest result to date has been reaching the top position in the company and completely rebuilding our credit and financial life. We are now able to save money again and pay for private school. We closed on our first Juice Plus+ house this year. Another big result was that I have been able to produce multiple top position leaders on my team. It is the power of duplication. There are systems in place to help teach anyone how to grow a business just like I did. I also love the ease of doing this business around my family's life.

WORDS OF ADVICE: Be teachable and coachable. Never stop. If you stop talking about your passion in your products, people will think you are done. This business is more personal growth than anything else you will do in life so be willing to change if you want your business to change.

Beth went from being in foreclosure and her confidence totally shattered to becoming a super star and inspiration in her company. No matter what your current circumstance may be, you can create success in this profession. Not only that but you can inspire those that don't believe they have any hope! Your story has certainly inspired us Beth and we are confident that in sharing your story you are showing thousands of others that they can have hope too.

NAME: Kelly Ellis-Neal

YEARS STARTED IN NETWORK MARKETING: 2009

PROFESSIONAL BACKGROUND: Landscaper and Commercial Truck Driver

COMPANY: Pure Romance

JOINED CURRENT COMPANY: 2014

HOW DID YOU FIND OUT ABOUT YOUR COMPANY?: The company I was formerly with was bought out by Pure Romance and I couldn't be happier about it. Other than my wedding day and the birth of my son it was the best day of my life. Totally life-changing for me and my family.

SUCCESS STORY: Twelve weeks after being full-time in the business I was the top-seller in the company. I sold $44,000 of product in eight weeks and made 55% of it. That was the beginning of my journey. Since then I've been able to pay off my debt and did not have to declare bankruptcy. To date I have earned the top leadership position in the company, Executive Director, of which there are only a few dozen in the world and I am touring as a corporate trainer to educate, empower and entertain women worldwide. It's crazy.

WORDS OF ADVICE: Stop worrying about what everyone else thinks. Their opinions do not pay your bills. Your enthusiasm does. Do it with a smile. Love what you do. Live with passion. Take a leap of faith and it will come back to you ten-fold. The rewards will far outweigh the risks.

Kelly went from losing her $1.5 million a year landscaping business, because she could no longer work it after having a freak accident, and near bankruptcy to a top-level leadership position in her company and the opportunity to travel the world to educate, empower and entertain women in just a few short years. She joined up as a member initially before she decided to make a serious business out of it.

So remember building a business right out of the gates is not the path everyone takes. Sometimes life intervenes and all of a sudden you realize what a gift you have in your hands to build your own home business. When you work hard, have faith and put all your eggs in one basket you never know what will happen! You might just end up with a fairy tale life. Kelly, you certainly have, and we're so grateful to you for sharing your story with us!

NAME: Joy Vertz

YEAR STARTED IN NETWORK MARKETING: 2005

PROFESSIONAL BACKGROUND: I have an art degree and I am a professional photographer and photography educator. I own two full time studios in Milwaukee, WI

COMPANY: Jamberry Nails

JOINED CURRENT COMPANY: 2014

HOW DID YOU FIND OUT ABOUT THE COMPANY?: I was a hostess and once my party neared $1000 I realized that I could have earned the hostess benefits AND commissions had I been a consultant!

SUCCESS STORY: I originally signed on for fun and slightly impulsively because I love the product. My friends and family were incredibly excited and my network branched out beyond them so quickly. I ended up making a full-time income in my first year, working part-time which is very exciting.

WORDS OF ADVICE: Be consistent. Work your business little-by-little every day. This is not a get-rich-quick business, but it can and will happen if you work your business consistently.

Joy started off being a supporter! She hosted for her friend to get her product for free and then realized she could be making money in the process. This may or may not happen to you, but it's important to understand that no matter where you decide you fit in, you can always transition into being a part-time or full-time entrepreneur. Thanks, Joy, for sharing your success story. Amazing what can be built in just one-year!

NAME: Jessica Bowser Nelson

YEAR STARTED IN NETWORK MARKETING: 2010

PROFESSIONAL BACKGROUND: Waitress

COMPANY: Beachbody

JOINED CURRENT COMPANY: 2010

HOW DID YOU FIND OUT ABOUT THE COMPANY?: By accident. I was a huge fan of the home workout programs simply due to the results that I got in less time than at the gym. I was super tired as life had literally sucked me dry and my "coach" recommended I try Shakeology—an all-natural superfood shake. I signed up as a coach to simply get the discount. I had no idea it was a network marketing company. Thankfully. Or I probably wouldn't have joined. I saw her earning money and living a life of freedom and she was shy and reserved. I realized if she could do it, WHY NOT ME?

SUCCESS STORY: My biggest result was becoming a million dollar earner. I can't say I was surprised because throughout my entire experience, I have really learned what I'm capable of in life and really made it my mission to help as many people as possible realize the same thing. We are capable of far more than we imagine! So, it wasn't a matter of IF for me, but WHEN!

WORDS OF ADVICE: At the beginning, you will be putting in a lot of work with seemingly little return. But, the ones that stick it out and keep going and stay focused, those are the ones that come out on top. If it was easy, everyone would do it. Don't be easy. You were meant for amazing things!

Jessica started off just loving the product and decided to share her experience. This happens with a lot of product users. Fast forward less than 5 years later and she's on pace to earn over a million dollars a year! We're so excited for you Jessica! Congratulations on all your hard work.

NAME: Tracey Schwartz

YEAR STARTED IN NETWORK MARKETING: 2007

PROFESSIONAL BACKGROUND: Sales, Mortgage, Finance

COMPANY: Stella & Dot

JOINED CURRENT COMPANY: 2007

HOW DID YOU FIND OUT ABOUT YOUR COMPANY?: I went to a trunk show and thought it looked like it would be a fun part-time gig. Little did I know it would change my life!

SUCCESS STORY: My biggest accomplishment has honestly been my paycheck! It's proof that helping others really does help yourself.

WORDS OF ADVICE: Have fun, be consistent with your efforts and be patient. Rome wasn't built in a day but you will achieve your goals if you keep your eye on the prize.

Tracey was frustrated in the mortgage industry and now makes a high six-figure income in network marketing. Again, a common theme you'll see with a lot of top earners is they fell in love with the product. You never know what will happen when you are passionate about something. Awesome story, Tracey!

NAME: Rosalyn Powell

YEAR STARTED IN NETWORK MARKETING: 2009

PROFESSIONAL BACKGROUND: Associates Degree in Criminal Justice and a Paralegal Degree

COMPANY: Advocare

JOINED CURRENT COMPANY: 2010

HOW DID YOU FIND OUT ABOUT YOUR COMPANY?: From a neighbor who approached me.

SUCCESS STORY: It's mind-blowing to me that I am getting time back. My job was sucking the life out of me and I was too tired to do any of the things I enjoyed. Last month making $8,000 was just almost like a dream...it was 7 times what I brought home being a para-professional in our local school system.

WORDS OF ADVICE: "NEVER quit! It is easy to work and build this business when times are great and things are moving, but I truly believe this business is built when you are in the dips, in those moments when you think it's over because nothing's happening. You feel like there is no one left to talk to. That is when many people quit. If you don't...and you keep digging...you will always come up out of that dip into your next level of success....every single time. BUILD HARDER IN THE HARD TIMES. I built the majority of my business working full-time in another high stress negative environment...no breaks...no time...so IT CAN BE DONE if you have a big enough reason to work it."

Have fun, be consistent with your efforts and be patient.

Rosalyn has a powerful message. We always think about building this business when it's the "perfect" or "right" time. The reality is, life marches on and there is never the perfect time. Just do what you can in the time you have and you'll be amazed at what can happen! Congratulations Rosalyn on all your success. We're so happy for you.

NAME: Cherie Rodriguez

YEAR STARTED IN NETWORK MARKETING: 2009

PROFESSIONAL BACKGROUND: BS in Education, Public School Teacher for 15 years

COMPANY: Thirty-One Gifts

JOINED CURRENT COMPANY: 2009

HOW DID YOU FIND OUT ABOUT YOUR COMPANY?: Through a friend.

SUCCESS STORY: I started out with a $99 kit just like everyone else in my company. I can remember being scared to set up my first vendor table at a trade show back in Minnesota, but I didn't let the fear stop me. I went inside, set up shop and everyone loved the bags! Now just 6 years later I've made it to the top leadership position in my company, National Executive Director, and I've helped thousands of women build their businesses too. Being able to sustain my family with this income and retire my husband from the Army after 24 years of Service has been incredible. This opportunity is definitely NOT my mother's Direct Sales business that I remember when I was a child. I would never have imagined that this business would be able to provide for our family the way it has.

WORDS OF ADVICE: Be Present! Take advantage of all the training your company has to offer and engage in all aspects of the business. Listen to the

> *I would never have imagined that this business would be able to provide for our family the way it has.*
>
>

leaders in your company and on your team. Most importantly, sell a "WHY"…not a "WHAT." In the words of Simon Sinek, best-selling author of Start with Why, "People don't buy what you do, they buy why you do it."

Many men and women are able to make enough money to retire their spouse through this amazing profession. If that's one of your goals then run with it, because you only get one shot in life. Thank you Cherie for sharing your story with us! You're a super star!

NAME: Paulette Roy

YEAR STARTED IN NETWORK MARKETING: 1990

PROFESSIONAL BACKGROUND: Both my husband Ron and I have backgrounds in traditional business. Ron ran a large mechanical contracting company. We also owned and operated a travel company as well as a photography business.

COMPANY: Mannatech Inc.

JOINED CURRENT COMPANY: 1994

HOW DID YOU FIND OUT ABOUT YOUR COMPANY?: We were invited by the founder of the company to lead a team of leaders to open the East coast—Florida to New England. Within that first year we became the first qualified Presidentials (top leadership position in our company at the time) on the East coast.

SUCCESS STORY: After almost 21 years with Mannatech, I still get totally jazzed to watch a new prospect marvel at the amazing choices they have by becoming part of our team. By constantly reaching out every chance we get to support our teams and the company, we have achieved the respect and love of our peers and have been recognized as the top business builders of the year in 2012. What an honor!

WORDS OF ADVICE: Never before has there been such a need for everyone to consider having their own home-based business. While the traditional workplace job opportunities are shrinking, the opportunities for the entrepreneur are there for the taking in the network marketing industry.

> *Never before has there been such a need for everyone to consider having their own home based business.*

Paulette and her husband now have a team of over 20,000 people. They, like many others, built their way out of financial devastation through network marketing. If you are facing debt you can't pay with your current paycheck, consider starting a home-based business and using the money you earn to pay down your credit cards, student loans or other outstanding debts. You're such an inspiration Paulette!

NAME: Lisa Wilbur

YEAR STARTED IN NETWORK MARKETING: 1981

PROFESSIONAL BACKGROUND: I have two Associates Degrees: one in data processing and one in management. I've worked as a cashier, cocktail waitress, convenience store clerk and secretary.

COMPANY: Avon

JOINED CURRENT COMPANY: 1993

HOW DID YOU FIND OUT ABOUT YOUR COMPANY?: I signed up to sell Avon when I was 18 years old and newly married to a sailor and we were stationed on Guam. I wanted to work to have money of my own and thought of Avon since I remembered the Avon Lady coming to my house as a child and I didn't see anyone selling Avon on Guam already. There were others, I just hadn't seen them. Avon did not become a network marketing company until 1991. I started building my team with Avon in 1993.

> *I do not have the skills or background to be earning that kind of money!*
>
>

SUCCESS STORY: My cumulative earnings from my network marketing Avon team totals over $4.5 million dollars. I do not have the skills or background to be earning that kind of money! I have also earned over 30 all-expense paid trips from Avon including trips to the Mediterranean, Alaska, Hawaii and multiple cruises. I am constantly surprised how even being "Just the Avon Lady" can be huge if you decide it is going to be huge.

WORDS OF ADVICE: Be open to always learning and growing, personally and professionally. And buckle your seatbelt for the long haul, it will get bumpy—but it will be worth it.

Lisa started network marketing when she was very young. There is no "best time" to get started towards financial freedom or success. People have become successful that have built this business when they were 18, and 84 years old. It's just a matter of how badly you want it. Thanks for sharing your story with us Lisa!

NAME: Debbie Fox Sasek

YEAR STARTED IN NETWORK MARKETING: 2006

PROFESSIONAL BACKGROUND: Bachelor's in International Business to stay-at-home mom, to successful realtor

COMPANY: It Works Global

JOINED CURRENT COMPANY: 2006

HOW DID YOU FIND OUT ABOUT YOUR COMPANY?: My husband Dave and I had a chance poolside conversation with an entrepreneur, who mentioned a new product and asked us if we had a Plan B? That one meeting changed our lives!

SUCCESS STORY: In one word Freedom! In just nine years we have built a team of over 11,000 distributors. We are top earners in our company, recently sold our home, purchased an RV and are taking our business on the road! This could have never happened had we not said "YES," to looking at our Plan B!

WORDS OF ADVICE: Prior to finding network marketing, we knew that if we kept doing the same thing, we would keep getting the same results. We did NOT have the time (so we thought) to build another business. We heard the words "building a Plan B one night a week" and so we took a leap of faith, made the time and our desire for more kept us going! If you want different results and think you don't have the time to create a Plan B, I encourage you to invest just one night a week building your dream life. You never know what could happen!

Debbie's goal is to help people believe in themselves, start dreaming again and empower others to achieve financial freedom. She will continue to make her dreams a reality and bring as many others on the journey with her as possible. Way to go Debbie!

NAME: Tanya Aliza

YEAR STARTED IN NETWORK MARKETING: 2009

PROFESSIONAL BACKGROUND: Finance Specialist

COMPANY: World Ventures Travel

JOINED CURRENT COMPANY: 2013

HOW DID YOU FIND OUT ABOUT YOUR COMPANY?: Some of our best friends shared the opportunity with us and the rest is history.

SUCCESS STORY: The best part of this business is being able to fire my boss and live a dream life everyday with the person I'm madly in love with. We were recently awarded #3 Recruiter in our company out of 316,000 active members. I'm also able to show others how to have success with confidence.

> *Believe it's possible!*
>

WORDS OF ADVICE: Believe it's possible! I never did in the beginning and it held me back for a year. Create a vision and think about your dream day every day to help you to keep going forward. Become a product of the product and never quit!

Tanya and Cesar are now two of the top recruiters in the company. They help people every day with their marketing and branding to distinguish themselves as leaders in the industry and they continually grow their business as well. Thank you Tanya for sharing your story with us. You and Cesar have built an amazing business and we are so inspired by your success!

We'll leave you with one final story from Elexsis McCarthy who is the founder of Makeup Eraser, a new network marketing company. This success story is a little different than the others, but it's another angle we want you to see. She took a product idea she personally wanted to use, developed it, market tested it and then 'accidentally' launched it into a network marketing company.

Let's see what she has to say.

NAME: Elexsis McCarthy

YEAR STARTED IN NETWORK MARKETING: 2013

PROFESSIONAL BACKGROUND: Real Estate Franchisor

COMPANY: Makeup Eraser

FOUNDED COMPANY: June 2013

HOW DID YOU DECIDED TO LAUNCH A DIRECT SALES COMPANY?: It was a God-thing. I was designing the banners for our first trade show in June of 2013. I knew we had a product that was fantastic and I was excited to share it with the world. I was in a meeting just before the banners went to print and someone said to put on the banner "Distributors Wanted". So I went with it and had it put on. During that show I had someone who approached me and wanted to purchase 100 makeup erasers and be a distributor! I was beyond excited.

SUCCESS STORY: In just two years we've helped 7,000 people open makeup eraser businesses. Of that number 60% have been with us for more than 14 months. But it's not just that. It's the lives we're changing. One of our reps was a shy timid girl from Missouri, but she recently walked into a store and secured a product order of 200 makeup erasers and it was the biggest confidence-building experience of her life. It's always about people. It's helping them succeed and building a culture of positive support and recognition.

WORDS OF ADVICE: Multi-level marketing is the same as traditional franchising without all the overhead. Put yourself in alliance with a product you love and run it as a business. Utilize all the same training your company provides for you and soon enough you'll make as much money as the traditional franchise owner. Remember you have to pick the right company, love their products and know their compensation plan. The most vital thing is you have to be 100% confident in the product.

Elexsis took a leap of faith, put some simple words on a banner and today, just two years later, is running a large business of her own from home. Congratulations on all of your success these past two years Elexsis. We're excited to see how your company continues to grow.

We encourage you to take her advice and find a product you love, run it like a business, soak in the training and support the company provides for you and soon enough you'll be running a big business from home too!

The Truth Is

Building a successful business from home does not happen overnight. These women have put in countless hours learning the skills necessary to become successful leaders. They have stuck with their business and didn't quit when they heard "No" for the hundredth time. They were able to see the vision of what they wanted to create and despite setbacks, slumps and discouragement they got up each day and said "Yes" to their dream to create freedom for themselves and their families.

None of them were born with a silver spoon in their mouth. No one has special connections or was given special favors which led to their success. They all have different personal, educational and professional backgrounds. They all heard about their businesses in different ways and they all took different journeys to get to where they are today. They ALL SAID YES to being open and taking a look at Plan B.

That is the beauty of partnering with a franchise from home opportunity. You have a plan laid out in front of you that will show you the way to success. All you have to do is follow it! There is no right or wrong way to get into this profession. If you're ready to take control of your life then don't delay. Seek out your local direct seller, ask her some questions, and then take a chance and say YES! Maybe one day soon you'll have a story to tell us too!

CHAPTER 6

When You Already Have Another Business

"Enjoying success requires the ability to adapt. Only by being open to change will you have a true opportunity to get the most from your talent."

~ Nolan Ryan

So far we've talked about the importance of consciously shifting spending to support our local business owners. You've learned about the pervasive myths and real facts of the multi-billion dollar direct sales industry. And you've read about the opportunity to get involved as a consumer, a supporter, a hobbyist or a part-time or full-time income earner.

If you already have a business then this chapter is especially for you. Whether you're a personal trainer or massage therapist, a dentist or a doctor, a realtor or blogger I have good news for you.

Would you believe it if I told you that you already have what makes many people successful in this industry? You have a network of people who are already consumers of your service. You have the trust and credibility of being a professional on your side. You have influence and are respected and revered by many. To put it simply… people listen to you.

Here's the fun part. What if I told you that you can easily add in another revenue stream into your existing business with little to no overhead and no extra staffing required? Keep reading and I'll show you how.

Two Ways to Grow Your Business

As you grow your business one of two decisions are usually made. Either you choose to grow deeper or wider. Growing deeper means you are more interested in being known for just one thing and to be highly specialized. You are a realtor who specializes only in million dollar homes in Port Royal, let's say. Or you decide to go wide. You are a realtor who also stages homes for sale and does appraisal work on the side.

Either choice can produce growth. Both options still require you to show up and perform some type of service. You are trading your time for money whether you are highly specialized or you offer a variety of services. Most businesses operate on a time for money model and most people engage in this for their entire lives. It's how we've been taught business works.

We start out as an hourly employee making minimum wage at the mall. We work hard and eventually become the store manager and get a pay increase. We go to college (or not) and eventually hope to increase our value enough to earn more per hour and/or earn a salary with bonuses. That's the American dream, right?

Not necessarily. If you have to be there to perform a task and are paid for it then you are stuck. Time will run out and there is a limit to the amount you can charge. One attorney friend of mine said it's like having on golden handcuffs. This is when you are making great money and yet to continue making it you have to keep doing surgery, keep running your gym, keep billing day in and day out in order to keep the money flowing. You also may have a high overhead including staff, rent, insurance, and such to keep the wheels turning.

Where there is no time-freedom there is NO freedom.

Now I have one question for you: What if there were a way to enjoy what you do now and build a part of your business that did not rely on your time being traded for money? That would really be the American dream, right?

Of course it would. We'd be foolish not to consider this option.

Think of your business. What other services or products could you incorporate that would align with a network marketing company? Jewelry? Handbags? Essential oils? Protein shakes? Travel services? Start doing a bit of research on the products different companies have to offer and see what makes sense for you. Then it's just a matter of opening an account, plugging into their systems and offering it to your current client base. This is an easy way to create an additional stream of income.

Exploring Your Business Possibilities

Let's take a minute to brainstorm together some ideas that can work for a few of the businesses I've mentioned above. This might be helpful to you if you have an already existing business and if you don't maybe this is something you can share with a friend who does.

For Doctors – Being a doctor you have the respect of the community, a good salary and the chance to help your patients live healthier lives. You also have a high-stress job where you are putting in a lot of hours every week. We know that your mission is to maximize your patient's health, offer solutions and suggestions for treatment, and to increase their chances of living longer and enjoying the years they have with good physical health. Your patients come to you for help, are open to your advice as a trained professional and are already seeking solutions for their own well-being.

Here's a thought. What if you could incorporate a line of products to help your patients with their health goals? Would that be in alignment with your mission to help your patients live healthier lives? I think so! I recently interviewed Nicholas Messina, M.D. who did just that. He was a general practitioner for over 20 years and finally decided, after much skepticism, to trial a nutritional program himself and eventually (after eight months of piloting on himself, his family and his staff and after seeing his two nurses lose over 100 pounds) rolled it out to his patients. Depending on your line of practice, great companies for doctors to research are nutritional product companies, vitamin companies, essential oils companies and skin care companies.

For Retail Store Owners – Owning a retail store is not for the faint of heart. You are a master at stocking inventory, managing staff schedules, marketing and bringing in new clientele and overseeing payroll. The monthly overhead and number of hours you put in to keep your store running and profitable is quite a lot. What if you could purchase some of your retail from a direct seller and carry it in your store? By doing so you would be exposing your current client base to new products and opening them up to the opportunity to be a virtual sales partner with you. It would be easy to host a monthly fashion night to showcase your products and share the opportunity with your customers to build a business too. Depending on the type of retail store you own and the client base you serve you might consider looking at companies whose products are jewelry, handbags and totes, clothing, makeup or kitchen gadgets.

For Massage Therapists and Personal Trainers – You have chosen a very rewarding and physically demanding career. You show up early, stay late and often work weekends. Your income depends on your health and I want you to think about, in the previous chapter, the Plan B option. What if you get injured and cannot work as many hours as you need? What if you want to be able to stop working weekends and nights? How are you going to incorporate another revenue stream into your business?

This is the answer! Assessing your client base, you'll see they are certainly interested in looking and feeling their best and they are willing to invest their time and money to that end. This is a great population of people to serve because they are typically highly motivated and understand the importance of taking care of themselves. Like doctors, you might like to look at nutritional product lines, vitamin and supplement lines, essential oils and skin care companies. Try them out first for yourself and then, when you find one you like, open an account and start offering the product to your clients. It will be a win-win for everyone.

For Travel Agents and Realtors – We all love you! Looking forward to booking our next dream vacation or buying our dream home is exciting. With the proliferation of the internet however, people are doing a lot of their own research online which makes finding and keeping clients even more challenging. Plus, like doctors, retail store owners and personal trainers, you are still caught in the cycle of producing that next sale and finding that next customer. If you are successful (and I'm sure you are) you provide top-shelf service and consistently ask for referrals and have branded and marketed yourself properly.

> *Would you believe it if I told you that you already have what makes many people successful in this industry?*
>
> ∞

All of this work pays off for sure! What we'd like you to consider is asking what type of subscription service can you incorporate with your current client base? Would they be open to purchasing a travel membership to get discounted pricing when they book their next dream trip? Would you consider gifting your clients with a logo branded bag you purchased through a direct sales company and helping them host a 'welcome home' party for their new neighbors? These are just a few ideas and there are dozens more. What would your client also buy from you?

For Bloggers and YouTubers – Wow, you have taken on a great challenge building a blog or YouTube channel. Both of these career paths require a commitment to creating a lot of free content, continually building and engaging with your audience and keeping up active profiles on many social media platforms. All of this requires a huge time investment (and often quite a bit of money) before you start seeing anything come back in the door. I have spoken with many bloggers who have found this to be true.

The good news is that you don't have to wait until you have one million subscribers and can generate a huge amount of revenue on a brand sponsorship and you don't have to collect dismal amazon affiliate checks in the meantime. You are very visible and connected to your community and people want to befriend you. They want access to you. The challenge is doing it in a way that makes sense for you.

Can you build a way for them to get behind the red-velvet rope and work with you so that it is a mutually beneficial relationship? Of course you can! Join a network marketing company and notify your readers and subscribers that you are going to be actively building a sales team and they are invited to work with you. It's so simple. Imagine how happy and motivated they would be if you gave them the chance to not just work with you personally, but also earn money doing so. I can't think of anything that could be more profitable for everyone involved.

Four Keys to Consider

Here is the key to incorporating a new product or service into your existing business for all of the examples given above.

1. You must choose to partner with a company based on the interests of your current client base. Ask yourself what their goals are, where they spend their money and how else you can serve them. When you do this, incorporating the product or service will make sense to your current patients/customers.

2. You must trust the person you are partnering with to help you. This business is all about strategic partnerships and in order to shorten your learning curve and launch successfully you will want to have the help of someone who is experienced in the company you choose. Align yourself with a network marketing professional.

3. You must believe 100% in the products you are selling. Open an account and order the products. Try them yourself. Get your staff to try them. Is the quality as good as, or better than, you had hoped? Read the company website. Understand their compensation plan and ask questions.

4. You must consistently share and talk about the products or services and naturally incorporate them into your existing business model. Dr. Messina said he created a "Nutritional Questionnaire" which all patients filled out in the waiting room to assess their interest in talking about nutrition. You can do something similar. Figure out how you are logically going to tie it into your business.

> *The great news is when you partner with the right person you will have a friend who is invested in helping you succeed and they will provide support as you roll out the new service/product.*
>
>

When you focus on serving your community in a new way you will soon see that the additional revenue stream makes sense and you'll wonder why you didn't do it years ago! Let's talk more strategically about HOW you can launch once you have determined which company is best for you.

Again, think of this like you would any franchise. When you choose a company that makes sense for you, you simply open an account. You are then permitted to sell a line of products/services to your customers, and you are given systems to help you be successful. You are compensated as you build your consumer network and as you offer the opportunity for others to share the products with their friends and family too.

Picture yourself at the head of a line holding hands with 10 other people. Next to you on a table is a glowing ball of electricity. You've seen them, right? Touch it and it will shock you and that shock will travel through the links hands to everyone who is a part of the chain holding on to your hand through someone else. This is what you are doing in a business sense.

When your client Suzy buys your products, and then her sister, Nancy, who lives 500 miles away wants them too, you get a credit for the sale. When Nancy's neighbor Beth buys, guess what? It all trickles back to you. That's the power of a building a network outside of the four walls of your office (or outside of your website). Even though you have never talked to either Beth or Nancy they are now your virtual customers and your sales revenue has just grown.

Can you see that now? Good. Let's keep going.

Seven Steps to Launching in Your Current Business

Understanding the power of building a consumer network is one thing. Figuring out how to do it is another. Here are seven simple and practical steps to successfully launching a virtual franchise in your current business model in just 7 weeks. Whether you are a doctor, a realtor, or a blogger, this timeline will help you see how simple it can be when you just say "Yes."

Week 1 – Assess Your Current Client Base

If you've been in business for any length of time you probably already have a core group of loyal clients. Think about them and answer the following questions to build out a client profile. This will help you as you proceed.

- What is the general demographic of this community of people?

- What is their age, gender, median income, lifestyle choices?

- What are their main interests?

- What problems have they expressed to you over time?

- What do they spend money on regularly?

- What keeps them up at night?

- What problems can you solve for them?

Week 2 – Research Possible Companies

Every company has a culture of its own. Just like you would research the growth opportunities of Subway, if you were considering opening a franchise, do the same for any direct selling company you may want to get involved with. To find out more about various networking companies go to the Direct Selling Association website at www.dsa.org.

If you were approached by another network marketing professional to look at their opportunity, please take the time to thoughtfully consider what they had to share. They met with you because they would love to work with you to help you build another revenue stream for your business. Would you enjoy working with them?

Good questions to ask at this point are:

- How old is the company?

- What are their annual sales? Is this number growing annually?

- How many active partners do they have? Are they international?

- How does their compensation plan work?

- Do you like the culture of the people who represent the company? You can find this out by asking to participate in a private FB group for the company representative and see what is going on in there. If there is an event that the company is hosting in your area, make a point to attend and learn more.

- How are the products sold? Person-to-Person? Party/Event model? Do you need to carry product to distribute them or are they shipped directly to the consumer?

- How often would someone likely buy the products? Once? A few times a year? Monthly?

You know your business and clientele best, so make those decisions based on what you see fitting in with your business.

Week 3 – Seek Out a Strong Partner

Launching a new service can be a very exciting process for you, your staff and your clients. It is highly advisable to undertake it strategically with the right support from someone else who is running a successful virtual franchise with the company you are considering. They will be a key factor in how well your launch goes and how much support you receive in the long run.

You may decide to schedule a few phone calls or in person meetings. Choose someone who is a strong leader. If you have narrowed it down to a few different companies you may want to interview a number of associates to see who you like best. This could be the beginning of a long-term lucrative relationship that is beneficial to both of you. Choose wisely.

Good questions to ask are:

- How do you see your company fitting into our business?

- What support can you offer us?

- What additional income can we expect if we partner with your company?

- What do you like about your company?

- What challenges do you foresee in launching this type of business here?

The person you are speaking with should be able to answer all of the questions above and offer you specific ways they can help you. You will feel it when the energy is right. I am a big believer in that!

The great news is when you partner with the right person you will have a friend who is invested in helping you succeed and they will provide support as you roll out the new service/product.

Week 4 – Open an Account and Try It Out

In order for this to be successful you have to feel 100% confident that what you are going to sell is the best there is. Sign up and order your first set of products. Include your staff and your friends in this process. When I was considering incorporating a nutritional system with my current coaching business, I asked 10 close friends to pilot it with me. They were all willing to support me and gave me honest feedback and from that I was able to decide what to do next.

- If you are considering a party company, host a party for your friends or staff. Do you like the process and can see yourself hosting regular events? Are you satisfied with the quality and delivery methods of the products?

- If you are considering a subscription service, sign up and use it. Are you satisfied with the discounts? Is it easy to use and is it something your clients will use?

Partnering with a network marketing company no matter what your professional background just makes sense.

- If you are considering a nutritional company, pilot their signature program. How do you feel when you are taking them? Are you getting results?

- If you are satisfied with your choice then continue on to Week 5. If not, go back and choose another company and pilot it again. The model works—you just have to find the fit that seems right for your company.

Week 5 – Make a Decision

Once you decide to go forward, let your local associate know and schedule a meeting with them. They will help you plan a timeline to launch and help you enroll any staff members who would like to earn additional money as a partner with you. This option is great for many front office workers who will be helping you administer the new service.

When you get your core team organized your local associate will do the job of training everyone on the basic product/service conversation and how to sell. They'll also be trained to input orders and manage the administrative parts of the business. Again, this varies depending on what type of company you choose.

Week 6 – Create a launch for your new offering

All systems ready! It's time to launch. Because you have selected a company and a consultant in your area, rest assured that you are not alone. You have a backbone of support to help you get started, so be sure to collaborate and ask for help. If you have a staff, make sure to keep them informed and offer first to let them get in on the partnership with you. There are two ways to do this. Pick what seems best for you.

The Big Launch – This rocket is about to hit the moon. This launch will require you to more actively engage your base. This can be a lot of fun and will get this added revenue off to an amazing start. Now it's time to incentivize.

I've seen gyms offer a prize of a year free membership for their clientele who take part in their launch. You could choose to do a raffle or gift certificate. You can also use the launch as a way to introduce your clients to each other through a party or other event. It's a great way to help everyone feel connected and bring new clients into your business when you invite them to bring a friend.

The Soft Launch – This is for your business if you don't feel comfortable hosting an event for your patients or clients together. You can simply have the products available and start sharing them on a one-to-one basis. This type of launch is quiet and personal. It can be as easy as starting to stock some products to be bought on-demand or showing a catalog or sharing a sample. Your business, your choice.

Week 7 – Build supporting systems into your current business culture

Once you launch your first event and everyone in the office is comfortable with it, you will need to continue to build this area of your business to create a great source of residual income. This will include training staff to handle enrolling new product users and following-up to offer support.

Where Can You Get Started?

With over 4,000 networking companies on the market today, there is no lack of opportunity, that's for sure! It's up to you to pick one and start profiting.

The great news is that when you introduce a client to your products and/or services, and they remain an active virtual customer, you are still generating revenue from them each and every month, whether they walk through your physical doors or read your blog or not.

Partnering with a network marketing company no matter what your professional background just makes sense. It's freeing to know you can easily add another avenue of service for your client base and in the process create another avenue of revenue for your brick and mortar business with very little overhead to implement. That's just smart business.

The final three chapters we thought it would be helpful to provide a little bit of basic training to get you started on the fast track to success. Jessica will cover some tips about building your business with Social Media, I have provided some tips on S.M.A.R.T. accountability and we will close it out with Ray (Jessica's hubby) who has generously provided a 90-day game plan. Let's get on with it!

CHAPTER 7

The Importance of Social Media

"Why Use Social Media? Marketing is no longer about the stuff that you make, but about the stories you tell."

~ Seth Godin

Well said Seth! I used to be one of those people that always hated Facebook. I thought it was a pointless privacy hazard. I was worried about all the creepers out there and also didn't understand why in the world people would waste their time sharing that they had just eaten a grilled cheese sandwich.

My point is that the way most people use social media can seem pointless because they're not making money from it or creating strategic relationships. I told you already that in my first five months of building a networking business I didn't enroll one person. Until I taught myself how to work it more effectively!

Posting about how much you hate your boyfriend or that your favorite candy is Sweet Tarts may seem important to you, but the truth is no one else really cares. However, if you use social media strategically, it is not only a great way to stay connected with prospects and customers, you can certainly build your business too. Had I known I would make more money in a month than I had ever made in a year using some simple social media tips, I would have started taking it seriously a lot sooner!

Two Main Strategies to Build your Home Business on Social Media

Because social media and the use of it in business is still relatively new and often misunderstood I want to share with you two ways I have found to successfully build my business using Facebook and I encourage you to use them too.

1. Active Prospecting

> *Had I known I would make more in a month than I had ever made in a year using some simple social media tips, I would have started taking it seriously a lot sooner!*
>
>

The most common question people ask me when they first start a home business is "where do I find people to talk to?" My answer is that there are literally billions of people on social media, and specifically on Facebook, who are just one click away. Unlike 20 years ago where you'd have to look in the phone book or go door-to-door, in today's world there's literally no excuse not to build a business.

We have thousands of cold market contacts right at our fingertips. With the right strategy in place to reach out to them and lead them from just a friend to a business associate, there is literally no limit to your potential income. I like to call this the ability to "recruit at will."

What if I told you in less than a half an hour a day you could create a 6-figure income from home using social media?

That's exactly what happened to me. I've recruited over 150 people into my business using social media AND I did it mainly through this concept of "actively prospecting" which means proactively reaching out to people and creating relationships with cold contacts.

In my 10k social media training (www.10kSocialMedia.com) I teach step-by-step how to enroll more team mates and customers through scripts and a solid marketing plan using Facebook and I'd like to share some of those actionable steps with you right now.

Also April hosted me for an hour-long webinar when I launched my 10K Social Media program and I shared many more tips and strategies. You can watch the full hour at http://bit.ly/10Kformula.

A few key components of this system are:

1. Always let people know WHY you're messaging them or reaching out.

2. Never put a link in the first message.

3. Reach out to at least 10 people per day.

> *Curiosity is the key in all social media platforms.*
>
>

People want to feel special. In a world where the Internet is making things more and more impersonal, messaging someone with the primary goal of enrolling them into your business doesn't work. It creates pressure for them and makes you look inauthentic. Trust me, they will run the other direction.

Take some time to read through their page. Understand what makes them tick. Then reach out letting them know why you picked them out of everyone else. That way they feel special and you will get an entirely different response.

Reaching out to ten people per day is a great target. It may seem small at first, but in a year's time that means you'll have reached out to over 3,650 people who you've added as a friend and you've ACTUALLY talked to—not just hit the 'accept friend' button. If you figure the average person closes about 5% of the people they talk to, which is a conservative estimate, you will have enrolled 182 new people in your business by the end of the year! For most compensation plans, that's a really nice residual income.

My friend Terry was a manager of a general store out of Montana making $35,000 a year. After following this training to a tee he was able to go full-time in his home business in less than a year, and is now making a solid 6 figure income. All Terry did was print out those scripts, place them next to his computer and follow them every day.

The most important thing to remember is to be consistent, and always develop a relationship before going in for the "pitch." If you do this right, social media could end up being your #1 lead generation tool and money maker.

2. Attraction Marketing

Attraction marketing means you're attracting people to you through whatever marketing, posts or content you're putting out there into the social space. Ideally people see your stuff on a regular basis, they like it and eventually they want to be a part of it.

This is the strategy that people usually LOVE to try first because it's comfortable and doesn't involve directly reaching out to people. One mistake many people make, which comes from a place of excitement when someone starts a new business, is that they post a bunch of stuff about their company and tell everyone to "Join my team!" They figure it's the easiest way to promote the business with the littlest amount of effort and that everyone will jump at the chance to join. This strategy rarely, if ever, works. It's very ineffective and can actually turn people off very quickly.

The best way to start promoting a new business on social media is to take people on your journey with you and provide curiosity. Curiosity is the key in all social media platforms.

Instead of saying "join my team" or "buy my product," make them curious about what you do by posting pictures of you having fun and living an exciting life. Make THEM come to YOU. Put a little mystery in the mix.

A great thing to post might be a picture of you smiling at your computer and a caption stating, "I'm really excited about my new business venture!"

Or if you're wanting to sell more product say something like, "I can't believe I've lost 30 pounds with this new plan of action and I feel fantastic. If you're struggling to lose weight there's hope! I promise."

> *Activity and action are the solution to most problems in business.* ∞

Very simple statements cause people to wonder, "What is she up to now?" That's what you want! Attraction marketing combined with actively prospecting is the key to building a huge business on social media.

In the first module of the 10k Social Media Recruiting Formula I give you an exact blueprint on how to set up your profile so people start asking you more specifically about what you do. This one mistake, which most people get wrong, can easily be avoided. All you have to do is create more curiosity, be less pitchy and be consistent with your posting.

The Power of Consistency

Everything we've talked about in this entire book, not just social media, will only work if you stay consistent. Consistency is absolutely necessary to any business no matter what type.

If you want to build a huge networking team or customer base, setting daily and weekly goals of income producing activities is one of the best things you can possibly do. Activity and action are the solution to most problems in business.

Let me be very clear, this doesn't include sharpening your pencils or constantly changing your profile picture. I am talking about strategic INCOME producing activities, like active prospecting and attraction marketing. They are the actions that are going to make you more money.

Whether it's three people a day or ten people a day you're committed to reaching out to, be sure to stick to it no matter what and soon enough you'll build an empire. You can start out small, and work your way into bigger and bigger goals. Remember, a small step every day can turn into a mile.

This is by far one of the toughest parts for people, and where April's accountability coaching really helps big time. In the beginning when I was aggressively building my business, I was reaching out to 20 people a day on Facebook and posting all kinds of "curiosity" provoking status updates.

I was committed 110% even though I was going to school full-time and working full-time. There wasn't one day that went by that I didn't show my business to at least three people. Sticking with that level of intense, focused activity can be challenging and you may need a partner to help keep you on track. Luckily I had Ray to keep me accountable. So if you're serious about succeeding you'll want to build in support too. Let's check in with April and see what she has to say about accountability.

CHAPTER 8

The Power of
Accountability

"Accountability is the glue that ties the
commitment to the result."

~ Bob Proctor

I absolutely loved what Jessica had to say about creating a social media strategy that includes both active prospecting and attraction marketing to get your business started. She is right that you have to be extremely consistent to build any business. I have often found that to do this you have to build in a system of accountability so that you are sure to stick with it through the inevitable ups and downs of business ownership.

One of the biggest challenges with having a home business is that *you are home*. There are a lot of distractions to keep you from doing the things that you need to do to grow your business, like laundry piling up, kids who need help and dishes to be done. You might even be working another job outside of the home, while you're building your networking business which often means committing to working it during evenings or on weekends.

I'm not saying to quit your current job, ignore your kids and let your house go to pot, I'm just saying that accountability is essential to your success. Whenever I've accomplished anything great (or just gotten my butt out of bed at 5:00 a.m. to work out on a regular basis) it's been because I knew someone else was counting on me.

I have seen a lot smart and talented women whose businesses failed from lack of on-going accountability. We're all fired up when we start but as the work sets in and the motivation to keep going wanes who is going to cheer you on? This is what you need to succeed.

Conversely, every woman I know who has made it to the top of their company (or consistently worked out at 5:00 a.m.) did so through nothing more than surrounding themselves with the right people and staying the course even when they wanted to quit.

> *Remember*
> *BUSY-NESS*
> *does not equal*
> *BUSINESS.*
>
>

Accountability is S.M.A.R.T.

Accountability isn't a sexy topic like social media or recruiting. Yet it's the glue that will hold everything else together. When you don't feel like reaching out to ten more people and you are feeling like your goals will never come to fruition, accountability will help you stick with it.

It's important that you understand how to use S.M.A.R.T. accountability. This is different that S.M.A.R.T. goal setting which we've all used before (Specific, Measurable, Attainable, Realistic, Timelined). This type of accountability will help you accomplish anything you set your mind to do in business and in life while using the help of other people's support.

Let's break it down and see what this means in your week-to-week business-building life. I'm going to pretend your name is Jenna, and you are my accountability partner so you can see how this process looks when we use the formula: S is for Structure, M is for Motivation, A is for Action, R is for Relationships and T is for Trust.

S is for Structure

I don't know about you, but I am a Type-A person. I always have dozens of balls in the air and often have no idea which one I'll catch and which one will drop.

When I work at the computer I typically have 20 tabs open on my browser along with various other off-line programs I'm *working on* open in the background. I'm thinking about the next video I want to record or blog I want to write while I'm driving. I have no less than five books I'm reading at one time stacked up on my night stand. This is all true!

If you're at all like me you could benefit from a bit of structure. Right? So how would Jenna, my accountability partner, help me with structure? This is one way she could do it. Let's role play.

Jenna: *What are you going to get done this week April?*

Me: I have so many ideas! Blogs to write, books to read, videos to create, people to reach out to, clients to coach. Yeah! I have a lot to do!

Jenna: *What SPECIFICALLY is YOUR MOST IMPORTANT TASK to get done this week?*

Me: I think the most important thing I need to do this week is reach out to ten new people and follow up with ten people.

Jenna: *Great! I'll hold you to it!*

That seems logical, right? An accountability partner can only help you if they know specifically what you are agreeing to do. For the dreamer, like me, this is crucial to help me stay focused on specific actions I can take to push my business forward and not get caught up in the clouds.

Remember BUSY-NESS does not equal BUSINESS. You have to be S.M.A.R.T. and build STRUCTURE into your business through Accountability!

M is for Motivation

If you've ever dreamed big or tried to accomplish something great it's likely you've hit a slump in the motivation area. Maybe you hit it hard in the beginning then you slowly petered out. Maybe you readjusted your BIG goals and made them SMALL goals because you doubted that you'd ever accomplish something SO BIG.

> *Be S.M.A.R.T. and use accountability to help you achieve your own highest level of success.*
>
>

Grant Cardone says in his book *The 10X Rule: The Only Difference Between Success and Failure* that you need to set HUGE goals so that you are driven to accomplish them and then set a date, a cost and a level of activity you think it will take to accomplish it. THEN multiply it by 10. So if you think you'll build a top-level business in one year, assume it will take ten years. If you think you'll need $1,000 to do it, then assume it will take $10,000. If you think making 10 calls a week is sufficient, plan on making 100 calls a week.

Sounds crazy, right? It's all about expectations. Most people quit something NOT because the goal was too big. It was because they severely underestimated the time, cost and effort it would take to accomplish it. Don't move the target closer, just adjust your assumption of how long it will take you to hit the target and start aiming. This is why you need accountability! Accountability provides motivation when you are making call number 57 for the week and you still have 43 more to go, and you only thought you were going to have to make 10.

Here's how Jenna could help me in a moment of discouragement like the one just described.

April: Hey Jenna, I'm just calling to tell you I'm wiped out and I can't make any more calls.

Jenna: *Sure you can! Every "No" you hear is one step closer to a "Yes"! You know that, right?*

April: Yes, I guess so. I just feel like I'm never going to be successful.

Jenna: *You already ARE successful. Nothing on the outside can make you BE successful. It is a part of who you ARE. Maybe that's the problem. You're thinking too much about YOU rather than just getting out there, offering the opportunity to help people and letting them decide.*

April: You're right. Thanks for reminding me that my job is just to offer to help. That makes me feel better.

Jenna: *And I think you're doing great. Text me every ten calls you make and I'll text you a special quote to keep you motivated. Ok?*

April: You're awesome! Thanks so much! I appreciate you.

Surround yourself with positive people who can support you while you area in the trenches. They are your life-blood to help you keep the dream alive when you are tempted to kill it. Stay motivated through accountability.

A is for Action

Accountability without action is pointless but accountability with ACTION is powerful. You can see from building in structure to your week and staying motivated you are well on your way. This is where YOU are responsible to make it happen.

Your partner can help you stay focused and inspire you when you're feeling down but they cannot take the action steps for you. That's your job. As I said, to get my butt out of bed at 5:00 a.m. it helps to know that I'm meeting someone to work out, but I still have to be the one to sit up, lace up my shoes and head out the door.

Their presence pushes me into action. Knowing that I want to honor my word and not disappoint them helps me to do what I otherwise might not do. Here is how that conversation might go inside my head if I were to want to bail on Jenna, and skip the work out or not make the calls.

April (personal): I'm so tired and my bed is so comfortable. I think I'll just go back to sleep. Wait! I can't go back to sleep. I promised Jenna I would meet her at the gym for a boxing class. I have to go. May as well get up!

OR

April (business): I really don't want to make those 43 extra calls I said I would make. But I promised Jenna I would text her after every ten calls. What if I don't text her? I have to text her! Ok I'll start dialing. I know she's waiting to hear from me.

R is for Relationships

We all value the opinions of others we care about. Think about it. If someone you didn't know came up to you and said, "I hate you," and the walked away, would you care? Probably not. But if your child or your best friend said that you would probably feel some hurt.

This is why accountability works. When we care about someone, we really don't want to disappoint them. We want to give our best effort and we, in some way, want them to be proud of us. Make sure that you choose to partner with someone, or a group of people, who you respect and who you will want to perform for. Make sure you care what they think of you and that you are someone they can trust to keep their word. When you invest in a relationship you will most certainly get more accomplished.

T is for Trust

Every solid accountability friendship has built into it a high level of trust. This one benefit alone is worth more than you might expect. Through setting goals and holding yourself accountable you are learning to trust your word. This is often an underestimated angle of accountability. If, in life and business, you are continually saying, "I'll do that," and then you never do it, you are subconsciously training yourself to not believe what you say.

Did you get that? If you say to yourself, "I'm going to reach out to twenty people this week," and then you get busy and don't do it, guess what? Next time you say "I'm going to reach out to twenty people this week," your subconscious mind says, "No you won't. You didn't last time. It's okay—everyone gets busy..." So you have trained yourself to wiggle out of commitments and make promises you won't keep. This is serious business.

When you don't trust your own word you will have a hard time making progress in your business. Hold yourself up to a high level of personal excellence through accountability, learn to follow through and keep your word. Then you will start to build up enough trust where you will believe what YOU say and others will too.

As the saying goes, "The road to hell is paved with good intentions." Don't allow your own good intentions to go unfulfilled week after week. Be S.M.A.R.T. and use accountability to help you achieve your own highest level of success.

Six Weekly Questions You Must Ask Yourself

Since I believe in systems I came up with a simple set of questions to ask your accountability partner every week. The best time to do this is Sunday night so that you are ready, game plan in hand, to hit the ground running Monday morning.

This is especially important if you are limited on the time you can commit to building your business each week. Filling out this form will help you to be extremely focused and use the hours you have as effectively as you can.

They have been created in a particular sequence to get you thinking specifically about what your highest level activities are and then tie them in with what results you hope your actions will bring. Remember that it's always good to ask questions, to keep growing and to take time out to take care of yourself too.

To get a free download of this sheet to print off every week and use with your accountability partner or on your own please visit www.apriloleary.com.

THE *Networking* REVOLUTION

SIX QUESTIONS TO ASK YOURSELF EVERY WEEK!

1. What is the most important task to accomplish this week?

2. What is the second most important task to accomplish this week?

3. What results do I hope these tasks will bring into my business?

4. What is one question I'd like answered about my business this week?

5. Who can I specifically help this week?

6. What special thing am I going to do to take care of myself this week?

(c) 2015 April O'Leary • Download your printable copy at apriloleary.com

---

Committing to Accountability

I guarantee if you commit to yourself and find a partner or group that can help you, you will ensure your success in a very quick period of time. If you don't have a partner or would prefer to work with a group you can check out my accountability group at www.apriloleary.com/hive. We work every week with these questions as a group and you'll have the opportunity to submit them in a digital format.

You'll also meet successful women from a variety of companies who are working their businesses from home and are ready to support you. I encourage you to stay the course even when it's hard in the beginning. The rewards are well worth the effort.

Now that you can see the way to freedom and have chosen to align your intentions with S.M.A.R.T. accountability you're ready to hear from our special guest, Jessica's husband, Ray Higdon. He's going to share with you a simple 90-Day game plan to get your business started or re-started in a powerful way. Take it away Ray!

CHAPTER 9

Your 90-Day Game Plan with Ray Higdon

"You will never change your life until you change something you do daily. The secret of your success is found in your daily routine."

~ John Maxwell

We're super excited to include this BONUS Chapter with Ray Higdon, Jessica's husband. He's an amazing trainer of top leaders in network marketing and we're grateful for his support of our book. Let's hear what he has to say!

Hey, it's Ray Higdon and I am going to share with you a 90-day game plan to help you build your home-based business in 9 simple steps. You know **the most important thing that I can tell you when it comes to a 90-day game plan, is to stick to it for 90 days!**

Do you realize that most people don't stick with anything for 90 days? Whether they want to learn how to play the guitar, learn a new language or lose some weight most people quit before they are successful. It is so rare for anybody to stick anything for 90 days. That is the truth.

I commend you for having the desire to build a home based business. Home based businesses have changed my life and the life of my family.

I get to spend more time with my kids now than ever before. My wife and I travel all over the world. It's been amazing and I couldn't' have done it without sticking to a plan. That is such a critical component and it's funny that I even have to say that, but I do.

Nine Steps to Your 90-Day Game Plan

There are a few things that will greatly increase your chances of being right where you want to be in 90 days. You want to be not just in the game but winning the game. Right? So let's go through some questions and ideas together. Feel free to write in the spaces provided for you and follow these nine simple steps to your 90-day success.

1. **Why did I start a home based business? What was the point? Why would I put myself through this?** Take a few minutes and write your answer down.

_____

_____

_____

_____

_____

_____

_____

You know most people don't have a home-based business. What is so special about you? Why do you want to have one? Maybe it's that you are sick of having no money at the end of the month, maybe it's because you are tired of asking for permission to take your kids on vacation. Why is it? You need to **identify the reasons why you want to build a successful home based business.** That is so critical for you to stick to this game. It really, really is.

Now on to question number two. After you have identified your why and really, really dug deep to uncover your reasons for owning a home-based business you will have to identify the vision you have for your life.

2. **What is it that you truly want to move toward? Who do you want to become?** Go ahead and write that down now too.

_____

_____

_____

_____

_____

_____

_____

I've found that when I was able to create a vision of who I wanted to become it was easier for me to stick to my business for the long haul. You will likely find the same thing to be true for you. Determine who you want to become.

The third thing to consider is the alternative. Now what does that mean? Simply, ask yourself, "What will happen if I don't build a successful home based business?"

> *The most important thing that I can tell you when it comes to a 90-day game plan, is to stick to it for 90 days!*
>
>

3. **What are your alternatives? What happens if you don't stick with this? What happens if you don't take this seriously?** This might get

a little painful and that's okay. **Would you have to keep working a job you hate? Would you have to skip your family vacation next year or forego braces for your kids? What does the alternative look like for you?** Write it down.

_____

_____

_____

_____

_____

_____

_____

You see when I was at my very last job in corporate America I looked at my boss, and I looked at his boss, and I looked at her boss and none of their jobs looked appealing to me. I didn't want any of them. I saw people who were stressed-out. They were under deadlines. They weren't happy. They had no time freedom and for me, that just looked painful. I knew I didn't want to do that.

This is the practical side of starting to and sticking with a 90-day game plan. It might not be as entertaining or exciting as you had planned but it's the reality of what it's going to take for you to make it in any home-based business.

4. **Are you willing to really embrace the fact that building a successful home-based business is a long-term decision?**
   Circle one: YES NO

You know, I will be honest—in my first 90 days, I made some money in my home based business. But if I was looking at the amount of time I put it into my home-based business my first 90 days versus the amount of money I made, it really didn't make much sense. I didn't make as much as I was making in corporate America. I didn't make as much as I had made in other jobs. I really didn't make that much.

Listen to this! My entire working life I had never made $10,000 in one month, but on month five of working hard in my home-based business, I had my first $10,000 month. It's important to realize that I had to stick with it, without seeing huge results, for more than 90-days. In fact, I suggest sticking with it for at least a year. But let's take it one step at a time.

Even if your goal isn't monetary, maybe you want to create some freedom in your life or create some other types of options, realize you still have to be willing to commit.

5. **Embrace a do-able, I am going to stress 'do-able', daily routine.**

I've taught about the importance of a daily routine for years and the only people that stick with a daily routine are the people that have a vision and fully know why they are doing this business. So if you haven't clarified that yet for yourself please go back and do it now.

Now why do I say do-able when talking about a daily routine? Here's an analogy to help you understand what I mean.

Let's pretend you know someone who is over-weight and out of shape. The New Year comes and they decide this is the year they are going to get back into their size 6 clothes. They start out with a bang, join a gym and decide to work out twice a day. Weights in the morning, cardio in the evening. The get their bag ready and head out the door. Just wait!

On day five they are going to be crippled with lactic acid. They are going to be paralyzed with soreness. They overdid it and now they need to recover. "Tomorrow, I'll go," they say. Now they are not as motivated and life starts getting busy again. They get back to their same old habits and forget about their membership. Although their goal to lose weight and get healthy was noble their plan simply wasn't do-able.

It would have been so much smarter and easier to take a long-term approach realizing they are not in shape now and that any healthy lifestyle change is just that, a lifestyle, not a quick fix. They could start on day one with just 15 minutes of walking or riding on the exercise bike and increase from there. Of course they could get an accountability buddy too!

6. **Focus on having conversations and sharing your product, service or opportunity every day.**

This IS your profit producing activity and the most important thing that you need to commit to each and every day. If you have a full-time job and you have three kids running around at home, you might decide to reach out to two to five people per day and see their openness about checking out what you are doing with either the product, the service or the opportunity.

> *Even if your goal isn't monetary, and you prefer to create some freedom in your life or create some other types of options, realize you still have to be willing to commit.*
>
>

That doesn't sound like very many people per day, but over the period of 90 days you will have spoken with 180 people. 180 people!

If you're brand new to this whole thing and maybe you don't have a lot of rapport you might get 5% of the people you talk to who will show interest in your product or joining your opportunity. That means over the course of 90 days you might have built a team of 9 people. Not bad! A lot of people would love to have 9 people in 90 days and that's just an estimation based on typical beginner results at the rate of talking with 2 people a day. What else should you commit to?

7. **Improve upon yourself each and every day, whatever that looks like for you.**

I often choose to vary what I do to invest in myself and my own personal growth. Right now, I listen to 30 minutes of audio books every single day, no matter what. I may also decide to take a course. I may attend a webinar. I may read a book. But at the very minimum I am listening to 30 minutes a day of an audio book.

What about you? What are you going to do every day to improve your life? You might choose meditation, reading, journaling, listening to books, attending online classes or trainings or following successful people online. No matter what you choose, please do some kind of self-improvement each and every day.

8. **If you are in a network marketing company, commit to attending your company events.**

Find out if there are any company events going on and get your butt to them. Yes, they are a commitment. Yes, you have to cover your own travel. Yes, there are associated expenses. Yes, you may have to work around a kennel or a babysitter or enlist the help of your spouse or an ex-spouse, right?

People who go to company events are more successful. And realize that everyone who attends has made sacrifices to be there. We all have to work around things but it's 100% worth it. There is no one in network marketing that creates a large business that doesn't attend their company events so make sure you do as well.

There is nothing like the power of being in a room with other people who share your vision and are working hard to make their dreams a reality too.

9. **Make sure that you pay attention to what is going on in your organization. Listen to your up-line and seek out others who can help you.**

That is the most amazing thing about network marketing. People care. They genuinely care about helping you succeed. So there is no excuse not to seek out the help of a sponsor, mentor, or coach to help you grow yourself and your business. There are others who have traveled the path you are on right now and it is your job to ask for help. Everyone who is successful deliberately puts themselves around people who are smarter and more successful than they are and then they soak up the knowledge and apply it into their businesses.

There you go. Super simple. Super easy. A 90-day game plan for you. I wish you the very, very best and I hope that this has been beneficial to you. Thanks so much. To sign up for the full 90-day game plan with me please visit http://www.topearner.com/90Days.

All the Best, Ray Higdon

Where Do You Go From Here?

We hope you enjoyed this book and that you will make a conscious commitment to support the women you know who have home-based business. Remember to write down their names in the back of this book.

Most importantly, we hope you will consider the benefits of starting a home business. Use this book as a tool to share this powerful message of opportunity with others who are looking for a simple path to home business ownership.

If this is you I encourage you to think it through and answer the questions below. See if you surprise yourself!

1. What I could gain by starting a home-based business.

2. What I might have to endure if I don't start a home-based business.

3. What is the biggest risk I'm taking if I started a home-based business?

4. What is the biggest payoff I could imagine if I were running a successful home-based business?

There are so many companies with such a variety of product lines and services that we are confident one will strike your fancy. Realize that there are thousands of women already on this home-business journey who are here to support you and help you succeed. We trust that you will find as much friendship, camaraderie, and value as we have in building a home-based business.

RESOURCES

Gifts, Courses, Websites and Videos

We hope you have found the information in this book to be insightful, educational and fun. We have included a lot of resources along the way and wanted to provide an easy place for you to reference them and sign up to get started. We encourage you to take advantage of doing your own research and educating yourself further through the links provided. Most of all, have fun!

#1 DOWNLOAD THE HOME BUSINESS MATRIX TODAY at www.TheNetworkingRevolution.com

---

Other Free Resources

29 Sources of Leads – www.RayHigdon.com

10K per Month from Facebook – www.JessicaHigdon.com

6 Questions to Ask Yourself Each week – www.AprilOLeary.com

Courses to Grow Your Business Quickly

The Hive Accountability Coaching Group – www.apriloleary.com/hive

10K Social Media Recruiting Formula – www.jessicahigdon.com/10ksocialmedia/

Your First 90 Days – http://www.topearner.com/90Days

Websites to Explore

The Direct Sellers Association – www.dsa.org

World Federation of Direct Selling Associations – http://www.wfdsa.org/

Direct Selling News – http://directsellingnews.com/

Videos to Watch

Is Network Marketing a Scam with Ray Higdon – http://rayhigdon.com/uh-oh-is-mlm-a-scam/

Direct Selling Endorsed by President Bill Clinton – http://www.apriloleary.com/clinton/

Facebook Recruiting with Jessica Higdon and April O'Leary – http://bit.ly/10Kformula

ACTIVITY

Seek and Find Your Local Direct Sellers

Your Guide to Supporting Local Women Entrepreneurs

This is your final stop on the journey to home business success. The more you support others the more you'll receive support in your business. Even if you choose not to have a business you can deliberately choose to be a conscious consumer.

Use this section of the book as a place to write down the contact information of women you meet who have their own businesses. The following are some general categories where you will find women who have direct sales businesses. Be on the lookout and try to get each category filled in! Then the next time you need something of this nature reach out to them first.

ACCESSORIES _____

_____

BAGS AND PURSES _____

_____

BATH AND BODY _____

_____

CANDLES _____

_____

CLOTHES _____

_____

FOOD PRODUCTS _____

_____

JEWELRY _____

_____

KITCHEN GADGETS _____

_____

MAKE-UP _____

_____

NUTRITIONAL PRODUCTS _____

_____

TRAVEL _____

_____

Lightning Source UK Ltd.
Milton Keynes UK
UKOW05f1121031216
289103UK00025B/946/P